COMMUNITY COLLEGES

AND ECONOMIC DEVELOPMENT:

MODELS OF INSTITUTIONAL EFFECTIVENESS

By

Stephen G. Katsinas

and

Vincent A. Lacey

© All rights reserved by the American Association of Community and Junior Colleges, One Dupont Circle, N.W., Suite 410, Washington, D.C. 20036. No part of this book can be reproduced in any form without written permission from AACJC and its representatives.

Printed in the U.S.A. 1989

IBSN 0-87117-202-X

TABLE OF CONTENTS

    Page

Foreword i

Acknowledgments iii

Introduction 1

Part One:
    Economic Development as It Applies to Community Colleges 4

    A.   Community College Emphasis on Economic Development in the 1980s 6

    B.   Traditional and Nontraditional Involvement by Community Colleges in Economic Development: Distinguishing Characteristics 10

Part Two:
    Trends and Forces Motivating Community College Involvement in Nontraditional Economic Development 13

    A.   Why Community Colleges are Expected to Provide Leadership in Economic Development 13

    B.   Community Colleges: A Delivery System in Place to Serve Local, State, and National Needs 14

    C.   The Economic Disruption of the 1980s 17

    D.   Community Colleges and America's Human Resource Development Crisis 22

    E.   Community Colleges and Shortcomings in American Political Ideology 24

Part Three:
    Seven Models of Nontraditional Involvement by Community Colleges in Economic Development 26

    A.   The Institute for Business and Industry at Lake Michigan College ... 26

    B.   The Mid-Florida Research and Business Center, Inc., at Daytona Beach Community College 30

    C.   The Pueblo Business Assistance Network at Pueblo Community College 33

		Page
D.	The Office Automation Center at Trident Technical College, Charleston, South Carolina	37
E.	Performance-Based Contracting, Florida Community College at Jacksonville	39
F.	The Bevill Center for Advanced Technology at Gadsden State Community College (Gadsden, Alabama)	43
G.	The Center for Business and Industry at Miami-Dade Community College: The International Dimension	49

Part Four:
Community College Involvement in Nontraditional Economic Development .. 55

A.	Impacts of and Motivation for Involvement of Seven Selected Community Colleges in Economic Development: Discussion and Analysis	55
B.	Common Factors that Appear to Lead to Success in Nontraditional Economic Development: Implications for Policy and Practice	60
C.	Nontraditional Economic Development at Community Colleges	66
D.	The Emerging Role of Community Colleges in Economic Development	68

A Concluding Thought: Look Before You Leap 73

Bibliography 74

FOREWORD
by
William F. Winter

In an era of unparalleled change in both the techniques and objectives of economic development, the role of America's community, junior, and technical colleges has never been so vital. Increasingly recognized by political and business leaders for their unique capabilities, these institutions in the decade of the 1980s have had thrust upon them a myriad of missions looking to the solution of the nation's social, economic, and education problems.

There is nothing particularly new about this except that now so much depends on the success of these efforts. In addition, the burden of expectations is equalled only by the increased complexity of the process. Conceived in a simpler time, these grass-roots institutions were for many years largely unappreciated step-children of an older and more sophisticated educational hierarchy. Much of that has changed. Under the press of economic necessity, there is now beginning to develop a maturing partnership relation between the two-year schools and the nation's four-year colleges and universities. More than that, there is now almost certainly in place that partnership between the community and technical colleges and private business and industry.

It is in addressing the innovative projects that are springing up in every area of the country that the most exciting and rewarding contributions by these institutions are now being made. In almost every state there are dramatic stories of educational and economic progress arising out of this enlarged mission. It should be only the beginning of a whole new era of constructive change built around the community colleges.

This very fact of their new-found success suggests, however, a time of special assessment and appraisal. Where once it may have been possible for community colleges, particularly those tucked away in isolated communities, to operate on a lower standard of accountability, now they must meet the competition not just on a local or regional basis but on a national and even a global scale.

That is why this volume represents such a valuable addition to our understanding of the new realities. We are now faced with a challenge unlike any that we have confronted in our history as a nation. That challenge involves our ability to create a more flexible and competitive work force. No longer is it possible for the country to compete effectively on the world scene with perhaps as many as twenty-five million of our adult population functionally illiterate. No longer can we pretend that a worker is set for life if he learns to do an initial job.

There must be a sense of urgency that attaches to the creation of a national resolve to make the investments in human resources that will enable us to be more competitive in the future. There must be a recognition that only through a matching of human skills and innovative business formation can we produce the real wealth that our economic system must have to meet its responsibilities.

The so-called military-industrial complex is not going to solve those social and economic problems. An artificial mood that causes us to feel good about ourselves but that is not accompanied by a serious commitment to increasing our knowledge and enhancing our skills is no panacea. A naive approach that ignores the growing disparity between the haves and the have-nots will almost certainly lead to a divisiveness and instability that will threaten our security as a nation.

Where then are the answers? Many of them obviously lie, as this volume suggests, in the nontraditional economic development strategies embraced in the great community college network. Only a few examples of some of the best are presented, but the ideas for replication and refinement abound. It will be out of the creativity and resourcefulness suggested in this study that true and certain strides will be made.

This task is too vital and too important to be left just to the professional educators. There must be a major leadership role in this development process by the public policymakers, business leaders, and sensitive citizen and community spokesmen. The network is in place, the ideas are being formulated, and the challenge is now.

As I travel across the country, I become increasingly aware of the strength that exists out there in the rank and file of American communities, many of them quite small and undistinguished. Harnessing that raw human power in a way that makes us a stronger nation is the task that is before us, and that represents a singular opportunity for the community, junior, and technical college system. As this volume suggests, the time has come for the country to recognize more fully the still untapped strength that it has in the resources of this national network of community institutions. How well we use them will determine how well we compete in the future.

> The Honorable William F. Winter
> Former Governor of Mississippi,
> Chairman, Southern Growth Policies Board
>   Commission on the Future of the South,
> Chairman, Mississippi Junior College
> Economic Development Foundation.

ACKNOWLEDGMENTS

This work rose directly from the work of Stephen G. Katsinas with the 41 publicly-controlled community, junior, and technical colleges while directing the Institute of Higher Research and Services of the University of Alabama from 1985 to 1987, and the long-term research interest of Vincent A. Lacey regarding higher education and economic development.

At the University of Alabama, the support of Dr. Joab L. Thomas, former President, Dr. James P. Curtis, Assistant Dean of the College of Education, and Ms. Mary Jolley, Director of Economic and Community Affairs under Vice President for External Affairs Dr. Malcolm Portera was sincerely appreciated and will be long remembered. The authors also wish to express their thanks to former Mississippi Governor William F. Winter for his thoughtful foreword, and to Professors Raymond Young of Washington State University and Ken Kempner of the University of Oregon for reviewing the manuscript and offering insightful comments. A special note of thanks is acknowledged to the project directors and presidents of each of the seven "model" institutions for their cooperation and openness in discussing the issues, problems, challenges, and options regarding the involvement of their community colleges in the arena of nontraditional economic development activities. Appreciation is acknowledged to Dr. Blanche Sloan and David Canine, former presidents of the National Council for Resource Development, for their support of the presentation of this research at various NCRD meetings. The authors also wish to express thanks to Jim Palmer, Vice President of Communications for AACJC, and Susan Reneau, Coordinator of Marketing and Publications for AACJC, for assistance with the manuscript, and Vera Felts for her highly professional assistance in the typing of the manuscript. Dr. Horace J. Traylor, Vice President of Institutional Advancement at Miami-Dade Community College, and Dr. John S. Jackson, Dean of the College of Liberal Arts at Southern Illinois University, are acknowledged for their support of this research. The responsibility for any errors is borne by the authors alone.

INTRODUCTION

Dramatic, dynamic economic and societal changes, especially since 1980, have challenged America's 1,200 community, junior, and technical colleges to redefine their missions, programs, and services. New and different students possessing diverse learning needs now populate the campuses, desirous of and needing more individualized instruction. In an environment characterized by change as perhaps the only constant, the topic of economic development and higher education has emerged to capture the interest, attention, and imagination of two- and four-year college institutional leaders; members of lay governance boards; administrative staffs of state, regional, and national higher education coordinating boards and agencies; governors; legislators; and the public alike. So captivating has been the attention that it is now rare to find a new college president who does not emphatically proclaim upon assuming office a "strong commitment" to economic development.

The trend toward more direct involvement by colleges and universities in economic development will likely grow and intensify. There are a variety of reasons, many interrelated, that provide an explanation for the phenomenal interest. These include:

- changing demography

- an economic landscape radically changed since 1975, the end of American involvement in the Vietnam War

- uneven economic recovery since the deep recession of 1979-1982

- "America's human resource development crisis," which describes the inadequate, noncompetitive set of job training/employment assistance programs and policies

- a failure of ideology on the part of America's political leadership that has led to intransigence and inaction, as opposed to solutionseeking.

Community college leaders need a general framework to understand the longer-term demographic, economic, political, and social trends that will impact upon institutional response to local needs. Advanced here is the premise that longer-term forces are dramatically changing the world of work, presenting great opportunities for community colleges--democracy's colleges--to serve business and industry, as well as the public sectors, in new and innovative ways.

Community colleges, particularly those in metropolitan areas, have been involved with economic development since well before World War I. Henry Ford Community College in Dearborn, Michigan, is an example. Chicago community colleges survived the 1930s by offering job-related preparation geared to the economic development needs of the area. Many of the state community college systems grew out of vocational institutes and schools. Much of the motivation for establishment of new community colleges during the late 1950s and the 1960s stemmed from a desire of local chambers of commerce, service organizations, and officials to enhance local economic development. These educational institutions typically had as their primary purpose providing well-trained technical workers to support growing heavy manufacturing industries. This was accomplished through the provision of formalized training for apprenticeship and quasi-apprenticeship trades, including electrical, auto mechanic, plumbing, and construction trades. In fact, a good part of the impetus behind the mushrooming community college movement of the era from 1955 to 1973 can be attributed to the critical shortage of technically trained workers combined with the baby-boom phenomenon. Over time, the community college achieved a position unequalled in American society, an open access institution that offered not only the tools of mid-management and technical types of employment, but also the tools of citizenship for more fully participating in democratic affairs.

In many ways the community college has come of age, achieving new respect and dignity within the field of higher education and the general public. These institutions will not remain static in the face of dynamic, sometimes disruptive economic, political, and social change; designing an entire postsecondary-level vocational curriculum around the training of skilled workers for declining and radically changed industries will not meet the challenges of increasing need for technicians, technologists, and mid-level managers and professional field workers. The simple reality that the typical American worker changes his or her occupation three or more times, and actual job six to seven times, on average over a forty-year span of participation in the work force speaks profoundly to the need for examining new nontraditional programs, services, and delivery methodologies.

The purpose of this monograph is to provide the reader with an overview of nontraditional, direct involvement by community colleges in economic development activities. While a review of the literature of community college economic development activities is provided, as well as discussion of the major factors leading to the unprecedented interest, the primary focus of this monograph is the presentation of the seven models of nontraditional community college involvement in economic development and the discussion of key issues, including factors leading to success that such involvement brings to the local economy. Thus, the approach is both practice-oriented and research based, designed to assist those interested in avoiding endless wheel-reinventing. Five research questions will be discussed in depth:

(1) What is to be learned from the literature regarding community college involvement in economic development activities generally and nontraditional involvement specifically?

(2) Why have certain forces and trends converged to make economic development a topic of such great interest to community colleges?

(3) What are some of the more prominent examples of nontraditional, direct involvement by community colleges in economic development, and how do they function?

(4) Are there key, identifiable factors central to the success that can be replicated elsewhere?

(5) What are some of the major problems encountered with implementation of nontraditional approaches, and how have they been resolved?

Part One of this monograph reviews the literature of economic development as it applies to community colleges and presents a model that distinguishes between traditional and nontraditional involvement of community colleges. In Part Two, key demographic, economic, and socio-political trends and forces are described that have provided incentives for community colleges to become involved in nontraditional economic development activities. Seven nontraditional models of direct involvement by community colleges in economic development are presented in Part Three by using a case-study approach. Key factors are discussed in Part Four that appear to lead to successful programs and problems involved in nontraditional approaches.

PART ONE:

ECONOMIC DEVELOPMENT AS IT APPLIES TO COMMUNITY COLLEGES

Since inception, community colleges have been involved in economic development of local communities. One of the major goals of community colleges has been to fill the needs of a developing industrial society, especially in the area of providing a skilled, well-trained technical work force. In the initial stage of community college development during the early part of the twentieth century, business and education leaders borrowed from the German educational system in establishing two-year schools with a special focus on technical training to meet the needs of the rapidly expanding industrial society in the United States.

A second stage of community college development in the United States occurred between the two world wars. During the 1920s and 1930s, educational leaders created a unique system of two-year colleges whose purpose was to provide job skills for the semiprofessional and technical fields, as well as to provide primarily low-income students with access to the first two years of college. In the early 1940s, many community colleges rapidly converted or established programs to accommodate defense industry and military training needs.

Following World War II, in a third phase of community college development, educational leaders moved away from the German model of two-year schools. Fearing the threat of communism, community college leaders, among them Dr. Jesse Bogue, promoted the concepts of "general education" and "citizenship training." During the mid-1960s and 1970s, educational leaders' goal for community colleges focused on training highly specialized technical, managerial, and semi-professional employees to meet the needs of industrial society; the 1980s have seen increased attention to ensuring that all citizens have access to education, with special attention to the needs of adult, minority, and nontraditional students (Goodwin, 1973, pp. 203-205). A thread of emphasis throughout the history of the community college movement has been the attempt to promote economic development through the training of citizens in two-year schools to meet the needs of local business and industry. This concern was paralleled simultaneously with a focus on students and fitting them for emerging job opportunities.

In *Economic Development and The Community College*, Long and his colleagues (1984) defined economic development as "the systematic, organized promotion of economic growth and business activity of all kinds" (p. 1). Numerous opportunities for promoting economic development in a wide range of areas have been available to community colleges. In the introduction to *Growth of an American Invention: A Documentary History of the Junior and Community College Movement*, Diener (1986) pointed out that during the twentieth century the community college "became a central figure in community discussions on how to create a new future, how to solve some of its problems" (p. 9). During the twentieth century, technological developments and work methodologies adopted by American industry created a new set of problems for American society: unemployment, under-employment, job dissatisfaction, alienation, and labor-management disputes. Machines displaced unskilled laborers, and business leaders turned to the technical and business programs provided by the curricula of community colleges to solve some of these problems.

During the latter half of the twentieth century, one of the most significant contributions made by community colleges was to provide training for the vocations occupying the middle ground between those of the craftsman-artisan type and the professions. An essential part of the community college system is the idea that each community college has its own individuality and mission, in accordance with its own environment (Lange, 1917, in Diener, 1986). Community college occupational education programs have traditionally been determined by the needs of the local community (Spanbauer, 1981). In 1947, the President's Commission on Higher Education outlined the essential characteristics of the community college system in the United States, calling for frequent surveys of local cultural, civic, industrial, and labor groups in order for community colleges to adapt their programs to the educational needs of local citizens, with a special focus on promoting economic development (U.S. President's Commission on Higher Education, 1947, 3:5-6).

In a speech to the House of Representatives in 1957, Utah's Representative Henry A. Dixon discussed a basic pattern used by community colleges for promoting economic development and meeting community needs. Dixon stated that community colleges usually take the following steps in setting up vocational training programs:

> [F]irst, it makes an occupational survey to determine positions available in the particular occupation being considered; second, it organizes an advisory committee of people engaged in the occupation; third, it develops the course of study with the help of the advisory committee; fourth, it installs the program; fifth, it places the graduates upon completion of their school program; and sixth, it supervises and assists those graduates to succeed on the job. (Dixon, 1957, in Diener, 1986, p. 152).

Throughout the 1960s and early 1970s, community colleges followed this pattern of action described by Dixon in developing technical programs to promote local economic development. At the first assembly of the newly renamed American Association of Community and Junior Colleges (AACJC) in 1972, one goal of the group was to "consider the development of occupational educational programs linked to business, industry, labor, and government a high priority" (Yarrington, 1973, p. 177).

Although most community colleges continued to interact with business and industry during the early 1970s, economic conditions following the oil crisis of 1973 and the ensuing recession brought about retrenchment on the part of some community college leaders. In an essay, Cross argued that the community college movement had lost its compelling energy and innovative attitudes. Cross concluded, "The goals that dominated college campuses in the 1960s are ranked very low in importance as we enter the 1980s" (Cross,

1981, in Diener, 1986, pp. 237-238). Cross also claimed that community colleges were working on rather "pragmatic, conventional goals," and she called for "clarity of vision and strong leadership to identify the new ideals that can unite and inspire to move community colleges off the plateau" (Cross, 1981, in Diener, 1986, p. 238).

A. Community College Emphasis on Economic Development in the 1980s

In the 1980s, a major goal of community college leaders has focused on economic development related to the "Age of Information" and the developing service industries. During the recession of the late 1970s and early 1980s in the United States, the industrial cities of the Northeast, Midwest, and mid-South were hardest hit by unemployment in the heavy manufacturing industries. In order to offset the lost jobs in the "smokestack" industries, community college programs were established to retrain heavy industry workers for the "Age of Information."

In the "Put America Back to Work" project, the American Association of Community and Junior Colleges took a lead role in placing two-year colleges at the forefront of national job training (Garrison, 1985). Eskow (1982) presented an agenda for community colleges to hold local forums on economic development in order to initiate cooperative efforts between business and education, to establish technology transfer networks, to assess community training and education needs, and to provide leadership in developing community economic development plans. In another essay, Eskow (1983) called for the establishment of human resource development councils at community colleges because community colleges were best suited to take the lead role in creating a national training strategy in the United States.

In the Northeast, Massachusetts instituted a number of community college programs to prepare its citizens for jobs in the semi-conductor, computer hardware, computer software, and telecommunications fields. Using the experiences of Northern Essex Community College, Brown (1981) outlined a model for starting programs involving local business and community colleges. In Rhode Island, although the proposed economic development plan was defeated, the Community College of Rhode Island successfully implemented apprenticeship opportunities, custom computer training programs, and other high-tech related courses to provide economic development in the state (Liston, 1984).

In New York, thirty community colleges emerged as economic development forces in their communities by providing more than 345 contract courses to 450 local businesses, especially in the high-tech areas. In 1980, the New York legislature provided the state's community colleges with the funding to encourage the contracting of courses that were unavailable under the older funding scheme. McGuire (1984) claimed that "New York's experience should serve as an example of how a relatively simple, nonbureaucratic, low-cost, statewide program can have a profound impact on corporate training. The key to success is the existence of a ready delivery system, and, in most states, that system exists in their community colleges" (McGuire, 1984, p. 74).

Along the Atlantic coast, nearly every state initiated community college programs to prepare American citizens for employment in the high technology industries. In Maryland, an imbalance between the demand for technically trained personnel and the ability of higher education to supply technically trained graduates existed, and efforts to correct this imbalance resulted in increased state funding for education in fields relating to high technology, mathematics, and science (Larkin, 1982). During the early 1980s, a number of community colleges in Maryland became active in establishing retraining programs in which business and education interacted. Calling upon the experience of Hagerstown Junior College in Maryland, Parsons (1985) emphasized the importance of the careful planning that must take place before technology transfer becomes successful, especially given the high equipment costs involved and the lack of expert instructors. In her study, Linthicum (1985) found that Maryland community colleges were successful in addressing the technological needs of local business.

In North Carolina, community and technical colleges continued the trend for preparing workers in the "Age of Information." In an article on program planning and economic development, Owens (1983) indicated that North Carolina community colleges had taken the lead in establishing cooperative skills training centers and formal internship programs between business and education. Between 1977 and 1982, nearly $11 billion in new and expanding industry investments and 170,000 jobs were announced in North Carolina, and Governor James B. Hunt, Jr., claimed that North Carolina's 58 technical colleges were the "backbone of our economy" (Owens, 1983, p. 55). In a related article, Robert Scott (1986-87), former North Carolina governor and current president of the state department of community colleges, traced the history of North Carolina's Research Triangle Park and its community college system, with a special focus on the interrelated roles of community colleges, government, business, and industry in fostering North Carolina's economic development efforts in the 1980s. In "No Shrinking Violet," Holdsworth (1984) claimed that North Carolina's community colleges were a major reason for the state's successful industrial recruitment.

Technical and community colleges in South Carolina have also played a major part in the economic development efforts of the business and education leaders. South Carolina's "Design for the 1980s" program is a customized training model for attracting new industry to the state (Bushnell, 1981). At Greenville Technical College, a network of industry advisory councils have been established to keep abreast of the rapidly changing computer and engineering technologies in order for Greenville Technical College to provide proper educational facilities (Barton, 1984). In an effort to establish better relations with local businesses, Florence-Darlington Technical College in South Carolina surveyed 121 local businesses and found that local firms were not employing many of the college's graduates; however, local businesses were willing to hire well-trained technical graduates with the ability to operate sophisticated equipment (Williamson, 1983). Additionally, Georgia's "Quick-Start" program is centered around the technical and vocational school system, and the program was successful in attracting TRW, Inc., a high-technology firm, to Georgia (Bushnell, 1981, p. 37).

In a report on community economic development efforts, Tyree and McConnell (1982) reviewed the literature regarding increased cooperation between education and industry for training Florida's labor force. They found that Florida's community colleges needed stronger governmental planning to provide training sessions at the work site and to contract training arrangements between community colleges and business. Jones and Beck (1982-83) discussed the accomplishments of Phillips County Community College in Arkansas. They claimed that a county-wide housing survey gave the community college important planning information which was used to expand the occupational education facilities and to foster county economic development.

With the closing of many "smokestack" industries during the late 1970s and early 1980s, state-level economic development programs became a preoccupation of state policy-makers in the industrial Midwest. The states of Pennsylvania, Ohio, Indiana, Illinois, Michigan, Wisconsin, Minnesota, and Iowa have all initiated programs involving community colleges in retraining workers who had lost their jobs in the "smokestack" industries. Learn (1983) found that Pennsylvania's community colleges' linkage programs with business involved customized training, utilization of industry personnel in the classroom, and practical work programs for students in order to promote economic development.

In a presentation at the Great Lakes Regional Conference of the American Technical Education Association, Groff (1982) described the efforts of Ohio's North Central Technical College to provide a computer literacy program. Groff charged that community and technical colleges must take a leading role in facilitating a smooth changeover to the information age by offering educational programs that properly train personnel to use the new machines. Groff (1983) also discussed the use of strategic planning and a human resource development model used by North Central Technical College and the Ohio Technology Transfer Organization in providing small business training needs.

Throughout the Midwest, community colleges have been called upon to retrain unemployed workers. The annual report of the Commission for Higher Education in Indiana identified three roles for education in providing economic development: (1) to educate and train first-time employees; (2) to provide in-service training for the currently employed; and (3) to provide research and development results to industry to facilitate planning. The commission also called for the establishment of a start-up fund to create new academic programs focusing on high-technology and the formation of educationindustry teams to learn from other states' research and development activities in the semi-conductor, telecommunications, and computer industries (Indiana State Commission for Higher Education, 1982).

Burger (1986) emphasized the importance of statewide planning in establishing the Illinois network of community college business centers. During fiscal year 1986, the Illinois state legislature allocated $3.5 million to Illinois community college business centers for economic development activities. Illinois community colleges provided training for 852 companies with 1,400 courses, serving 29,000 employees. Nearly 35,000 potential and existing business people were provided entrepreneurship training and services.

Additionally, the community colleges also assisted nearly 2,900 businesses in obtaining $39 million in federal contracts (Illinois Economic Development Grant Report, 1986).

In the "Keep America Working Project," the Sears-Roebuck Foundation established nearly a $1 million grant to community colleges in order to deal with the "Challenge of a Changing American Economy." Partnership project awards were given to Delta College, Michigan; Des Moines Area Community College, Iowa; and Metropolitan Technical Community College, Nebraska; for exemplary and innovative business partnership programs (AACJC, 1986). The major focus of the Sears Partnership Development program was aimed at permanent partnerships, especially in high-technology areas (Israel, 1986).

As one of the hardest hit by the recessions of the late 1970s and early 1980s, Michigan has been very aggressive in establishing community college economic development programs. In Michigan, community college programs have focused on retraining workers in microcomputers, word processing, statistical process control, and telecommunications (Delta College, 1984).

In a presentation at the annual conference of the Council for Advancement and Support of Education, Edge and MacDonald (1986) described four economic development initiatives involving Oregon community colleges. A "business incubator" partnership between Portland Community College and developing small business enterprises led to the formation of the Cascade Business Center Corporation, providing professional support services and educational programs. The Fisherman Technology Program at Catsop Community College provides technical training and information to fishing and marine businesses in Oregon and the Northwest. The ED-NET program involves fifteen Oregon community colleges in delivering specialized custom-designed educational programs via an instructional television fixed service microwave system to rural and underserved areas of the state. In the 2+2+2 Cooperative Honors Program in Electrical Engineering and Computer Engineering, Portland Community College, the University of Portland, and the Oregon Graduate Center cooperate with local high technology industries in designing academic programs to meet the needs of the growing informational services industries in Portland (Edge and MacDonald, 1986).

Throughout the twentieth century, community colleges have been and continue to be involved in economic efforts at the local, state, and national levels. Diener (1986) concluded that:

> Perhaps this is the most American feature of this American invention: that the community college is of the people, by the people, and for the people. It arises from the aspirations and faith of the people of a locale or state; it holds itself open to rapid change; it adapts and reshapes its organization and offerings in response to changing societal needs (p. 17).

Korim (1981) stated that "the trend of interlocking arrangements and other forms of collaboration between education and noneducation institutions promises to modify the profile of community colleges in the decade ahead" (p. 17). Indeed, community college leaders will need to interact closely with business and industry leaders in order to better prepare future students for the " Age of Information." The methods for contract training programs are well established in the community college literature, and new programs will need to be created to meet the demands of the high-technology and service-based industries.

The most important outcome of community college participation in economic development activities involves the students and clients served, the local economies, and the curriculum and faculty professional development within the institution. Community colleges offering post-secondary vocational courses are responsible for providing training on up-to-date machinery to the students served. At the same time, these institutions are challenged to provide more individualized instructional programs to an increasingly diverse student population. Rapid technological changes, however, are diminishing the ability of two-year colleges to afford the expensive machinery needed to keep students and faculty current with workplace practices. Active involvement by community colleges by definition implies in-depth research to assess local business needs. Through contact with local businesses and industries in the private sector, as well as agencies and organizations in the public sector, the scarce resources of the community college and the local businesses served can be more effectively employed. Thus, involvement in economic development activities of a nontraditional nature can open new vistas and opportunities for community colleges to be utilized to better meet community needs.

B. **Traditional and Nontraditional Involvement by Community Colleges in Economic Development: Distinguishing Characteristics**

There are significant differences between traditional and nontraditional involvement by community colleges in economic development. Typically, traditional involvement leads to an associate's degree or certificate of completion, denoting mastery of generalized skills and work methods, in length is a longer-term program, is located on the campus, and has self-directed participants attending on a noncompulsory basis. Funds to finance participation by students in traditional occupational vocational programs come from a variety of federal, state, local, and private sources. Direct responsibility for curriculum development rests with educators and curriculum specialists, and the locus of control is internal, attached to the community college. Figure One, "A Model Distinguishing Characteristics of Traditional and Nontraditional Involvement by Community Colleges in Economic Development," presents a conceptual framework for determining differences between traditional and nontraditional approaches to community college involvement in economic development.

Figure One: A Model Distinguishing Characteristics Of Traditional And Nontraditional Involvement By Community Colleges In Economic Development

TRADITIONAL	CHARACTERISTIC	NONTRADITIONAL
Associate Degree, Certificate, or Diploma	LEARNING OUTCOME	Completion of special/ customized training
Mastery of generalized skills & work methods	LEARNING OBJECTIVE	Mastery of *specific* skills & work methods
Longer term	LENGTH OF PROGRAM	Short term
Oncampus place	LOCATION	Often off-campus at work
Self-directed, noncompulsory	PARTICIPANTS	Externally directed, Sometimes compulsory as a condition of employment
Mostly full-time faculty	TEACHERS	Mostly part-time with tenured instructors & trainers
Directly, by educators/ curriculum specialists	PROGRAM/ CURRICULUM DEVELOPMENT	Indirectly, third party involvement
Variety of sources	WHO PAYS	Often single source
Internal, attached to the college	LOCUS OF CONTROL	External, detached from the college
By educators	EVALUATION	By delivery agent and third party
By institution and/or program through profession-specific and regional associations	ACCREDITATION	By individual curriculum specialist through certification
To locality and state through faculty, administration, and board of lay governance	ACCOUNTABILITY	To third party paying for the program

In sharp contrast with the traditional model, the nontraditional model's student involvement typically leads to completion of a short course and/or a certificate of completion that may or may not translate into credit, where mastery of specific skills and work methods is the learning objective, during a short-term program, located off campus at the workplace, with participants externally directed as a condition of employment. Funds to finance participation by students are typically derived from the client paying for the program or service, with some supporting assistance under the Job Training Partnership Act and from various state and local programs. Teachers for nontraditional programs typically come from private industry and do not hold tenure as full-time college faculty, while responsibility for program and curriculum development is vested in the coordinating unit or center in conjunction with the client organization. Thus, the locus of control for nontraditional community college initiatives in economic development is more external and detached from the college. One of the major distinguishing characteristics of the nontraditional approach to community college involvement in economic development is that none of the seven directors of the nontraditional projects described in this monograph was a member of the college president's cabinet.

In the areas of evaluation, accreditation, and accountability, major differences exist between the nontraditional approach taken by the seven institutions and the more traditional approach to these areas. Evaluation, the goal of which in the abstract is positive improvement, is performed solely by educators in traditional economic development activities; the delivery agent and a third party perform evaluations for nontraditional economic development activities. Accreditation is accomplished by the institution in the case of traditional activities, through the vehicle of voluntary participation in professionspecific and regional accrediting associations. There is no formalized accreditation for most nontraditional community college initiatives in economic development, although many teachers and trainers are likely to hold professional certification. Traditional programs are held accountable to the locality and the state through the faculty, college administration, and the board of lay governance, whereas accountability for nontraditional programs is generally to the third party paying for the program. While most of the economic development activities community colleges currently engage in can be categorized by the model presented in Figure One, some of the activities are not easily classified. Still, in sum the role of community colleges in economic training has clearly moved beyond the development of high-quality apprenticeship programs, which the above-mentioned model well describes.

PART TWO:

TRENDS AND FORCES MOTIVATING COMMUNITY COLLEGE INVOLVEMENT IN NONTRADITIONAL ECONOMIC DEVELOPMENT

Introduction

From the preceding review of the literature on community colleges and economic development, it is clear that these institutions have been involved in economic development as a central part of their missions for years. With regard to the nontransfer function, community colleges have departed markedly in recent years from the concept of educational programs and activities designed around skilled crafts/trades and the quasi-apprenticeship programs of the immediate post-World War II era. Today community colleges are directly involved in many diverse nontraditional economic development programs, including: centers for small business assistance and incubation; local and regional centers for planning; research, and information dissemination; office automation centers; programs providing customized training and retraining for business and industry, often offered at the plant site; performance-based contracting; the development of partnerships with universities, communities, and the private sector to provide advanced manufacturing technological assistance; and the promotion of international trade and development. The programs promoting economic development found at America's community, junior, and technical colleges are as diverse as the local needs.

There is a growing recognition among policymakers in the public and private sectors that community colleges are well positioned to help the nation deal with the various problems outlined above. This is demonstrated by the major helping role assumed by community colleges in states such as Michigan, South Carolina, Illinois, and North Carolina, which have been buffeted by major long-term shifts in the labor force. To provide readers with important background as to *why* nontraditional economic development is gaining in importance, this section presents reasons why policymakers at the local, state, and federal levels, as well as in the private sector, are looking to the community college to play a more productive role in supporting the economic development of their service areas.

A. <u>Why Community Colleges are Expected to Provide Leadership in Economic Development</u>

There appear to be five major reasons that explain why leaders in the private and public sectors are increasingly looking to the community college for assistance in developing creative local responses to changing economic and demographic conditions:

(1) Recognition of the community college as an agency and catalytic vehicle to provide assimilation assistance to new immigrants to a given region, in measure due to the recognized excellence of community college remediation programs;

(2) Recognition of the need for new directions to expand and diversify a given local economy in responding to the economic disruptions of the early 1980s, together with the recognition of the role of institutions of higher education in stabilizing and retaining a given area's traditional economic base, especially for areas with heavy manufacturing industries;

(3) Recognition of serious flaws in employment assistance/job training policies in the larger context of economic and demographic change, necessitating greater community college involvement in new and creative solutions, combined with recognition and awareness of the primary role and competence of the community college in providing training and retraining services;

(4) Recognition of shortcomings in current American political ideology that prevent community colleges from rising to their full capacity in economically assisting their service areas; and

(5) A growing recognition that as community-based institutions, community colleges constitute a delivery system already in place to provide new programs and services.

B. Community Colleges: A Delivery System in Place to Serve Local, State, and National Needs

Of the five prominent reasons that appear to be important in explaining why private and public sector leaders are increasingly turning to the community college for leadership, the last reason given is perhaps most important. With community colleges located in most of of the nation's 435 congressional districts, and with the substantial enrollments these institutions now possess within higher education, it is natural that Congress and the various state legislatures would turn to the community college for assistance. A more direct role for community colleges was envisioned by Congressman Terry L. Bruce (D-Illinois). Key sections of the National Higher Education and Economic Development Act, sponsored by Bruce in 1985, were written into the reauthorized Higher Education Act of 1986 under the new Title XI "Partnerships for Economic Development and Urban Community Service." While no monies were appropriated in 1986 due to the Gramm-Rudman-Hollings Emergency Deficit Reduction Act, the congressional findings and purpose make clear the kind of expanded role federal policy leaders see for institutions of higher education, including community, junior, and technical colleges.

Under Part A, Partnerships for Economic Development, Section 1101,

(a) FINDINGS--The Congress finds that--

(1) there is a need for more systematic and comprehensive efforts to link postsecondary education institutions with state and local

governments, labor, business, industry, and community organizations, in order to meet local problems and to plan, maintain, and attract lasting economic development;

(2) effective economic development is enhanced by the active participation of postsecondary education institutions;

(3) The economic vitality and international competitiveness of the United States depends on using all available resources; and

(4) Federal leadership is critical to promoting such competitiveness efforts.

(b) PURPOSE--The purpose of this part is to encourage the involvement of postsecondary education institutions with units of government, labor, business, industry, and community organizations to--

(1) conduct planning, research, and activities that promote economic development and the expansion and retention of jobs on the local, state and regional level;

(2) develop programs for job retraining and expanding business and industry opportunities in the area;

(3) enhance local growth initiatives through utilization of their expertise in economic and community development; and

(4) demonstrate new approaches to economic development partnerships and to make them available to other areas of the nation. (Higher Education Act of 1986, Title XI)

The foregoing reflects that federal policymakers envision a much more active role for institutions of higher education in economic development. This enthusiasm extends to state and local officials as well. In fact, few college presidents today are chosen without making at least some reference to the promotion of area and regional economic development. It is unlikely that the desire on the part of policymakers for involvement of institutions of higher education is not merely a passing fad. That community college enrollment is approximately one-half of all United States higher education enrollments and that most of the 435 congressional districts have two-year colleges are now well-known and recognized facts. As the nation finally moves to solve its human resource development, economic, and social problems, it is likely to turn to the community college for answers.

There are many implications for community college faculty and staff to consider in accomplishing the expanded role of community colleges in economic development. Child care, counseling, individualized learning programs for students possessing diverse learning backgrounds, student work, student outcomes and assessment, financial aid for part-time students, bilingual educational programs, services to improve the quality of life for seniors, and increased knowledge of the growing Hispanic population are just some of the more obvious and important implications. A brief discussion detailing the more prominent demographic implications follows:

- *Child care.* These services will become increasingly more essential if working women are to have full access to postsecondary education. Between 1970 and 1982, the number of women aged 25 to 29 enrolled in college rose 249 percent, while the number of women aged 30 to 34 increased by 314 percent, according to Helen Blank, Director of Child Care for the Children's Defense Fund (Greene, 1985). Currently, no programs exist within the federal Higher Education Act to directly support child care. Only 1,800 of America's six million employers provide on-site child care or employee benefits to finance such care (AASCU, 1986). Providing child care, especially in the evening, will be critical if women and working parents are to fully participate in adult basic education, G.E.D. programs, bilingual education, and developmental studies programs.

- *An operationally broader definition of student services at community colleges.* Student services will take on a role of increased importance at community, junior, and technical colleges. New student populations whose families possess little knowledge of complex student financial aid, admissions, and transfer processes desperately need and deserve expanded advising services. Traditional graduate academic programs in higher education that train community college student service professionals will need to incorporate a broader operational role of student services in the curriculum, with a strong practice-based orientation.

- *Understanding the diverse Hispanic student population.* Until 1980 there was great controversy regarding an actual definition of what constituted "Hispanic origin" from the Bureau of the Census. Now it is clear that America's fastest growing ethnic group has great diversity among and between the three largest subgroups--Mexicans, Cubans, and Puerto Ricans--which together comprise the vast majority of the Hispanic-American population. Faculty and staff can better serve these new students if sensitized to the social, economic, political, and cultural context of the Hispanic experience in American life. Particularly important if racial and ethnic stereotypes are to be avoided is the respect for and nurturing of the strong work ethic held by Latinos.

- *Enhanced opportunities for student work.* The complexity of the student aid forms themselves has been shown to pose a barrier to students from families possessing deficiencies in the writing and speaking of English. Nearly three-quarters of Hispanics enrolled in higher education are found in community colleges. Given the abysmally low rates of transfer for minorities and the proven effectiveness of student work as a retention technique, community colleges should work with the private sector to promote student work as a vehicle of college finance and overall worker productivity.

The ability of community, junior, and technical colleges to meet community needs has been underscored by the recent report of the Commission on the Future of Community Colleges, titled *Building Communities: A Vision for a New Century*. In a sense, the publication of this document indicated a coming of age of the community college movement, as its umbrella organization, the American Association of Community and Junior Colleges, initiated the report. *Building Communities* represents one of the first national reform efforts self-generated by the community college movement. In this 1988 report, economic development was prominently featured, as noted in the epilogue:

> One point emerges with stark clarity from all we have said: community colleges and the nation's future are inextricably interlocked. At a time when society's values are shaped and revised by the fashion of the marketplace, the influence of the community college must grow outward from a core of integrity and confidence firmly rooted in humane goals lacking in too many of our societal institutions. Future generations of Americans must be educated for life in an increasingly complex world. Knowledge must be made available to the work force to keep America an economically vital place (AACJC Commission on the Future of Community Colleges, 1988).

C. The Economic Disruption of the 1980s

The economics of the post-Vietnam War era are a second major reason why community colleges have received such great attention from policymakers in the public and private sectors. The period since 1973 is employed as a bench mark for two reasons: first, that year marked the end of U.S. Army troops in South Vietnam; second, 1973 was the year of the Yom Kippur Middle East War, which saw the use of an oil embargo that had dramatic global consequences. Both were watershed events--politically, economically, culturally, and psychologically, and together represented a clear break with the optimism of the quarter century following World War II. Presented in Table One are averages of the prime interest rates charged by the nation's thirty largest banks to their best customers, the rate of inflation, and the unemployment rate for the periods 1948-1965, 1966-1973, 1974-1980, and 1981-1988.

TABLE ONE:
SEVERAL KEY INDICATORS OF U.S. ECONOMIC HEALTH, 1948-1988

	1948-65	1966-73	1974-80	1981-88
Prime Rate of Interest[1]	3.91	6.34	11.11	11.5
Inflation[2]	1.83	4.13	8.76	4.6
Unemployment[3]	4.86	4.44	7.01	7.5
Federal Deficit	-0.1	-8.7	-40.2	-177.9*
Energy Costs	0.8	3.2	17.0	0.7*

*Estimated

Definitions

The **prime rate of interest** is an average of the percent interest rate charged by the thirty largest U.S. banks to their best, most credit worthy customers on short-term loans.

The **inflation rate** reflects a percentage increase or decrease in the cost of living.

The **unemployment rate** reflects unemployment as a percentage of the civilian labor force, and does not include the Armed Forces.

The **federal deficit** reflects the budget deficit or surplus of revenues and expenditures of the federal government of the United States of America in billions of dollars.

Energy costs reflect the annual changes in the cost of energy, which includes home heating oil, gasoline, motor oil, electricity, natural gas, and other household fuels. Data in the first column is for the period 1958-1965, not 1948-1965.

Sources

[1]*Economic Report of the President*, 1989 ed., Table B-71, "Bond Yields and Interest Rates, 1928-1988"
[2]*Economic Report of the President*, 1989 ed., Table B-62, "Changes in Consumer Price Indexes, Commodities, and Services, 1929-1987"
[3]*Economic Report of the President*, 1989 ed., Table B-39, "Unemployment Rate, 1929-1988"
Economic Report of the President, 1989 ed., Table B-7, "Federal and State and Local Government Receipts and Expenditures, National Income and Product Accounts, 1929-1988"

The structure of the American economy has changed dramatically since 1973, when the nation found itself convulsing from the higher inflation and interest rates brought on by the Vietnam War and the 1979 quadrupling of crude oil prices by the Organization of Petroleum Exporting Countries (OPEC) cartel (Bator, 1983). Like Great Britain in the days of King George III after its unsuccessful attempt to quash the American rebellion, America after Vietnam was sentenced to inflation. The Vietnam War was financed after 1968 almost entirely through deficits and a continual run of the printing press (Galbraith, 1975). To the credit of the Carter Administration, the *rate* of deficit was brought down in each succeeding year in office (Ott, 1983). Still, the high inflation caused by the Vietnam War and the hollow commitment made in 1973 to President Nixon's "Project Energy Independence" left the nation vulnerable to the actions of the OPEC cartel in 1979 and 1980 (Kuenne, 1983). As economist Ronald E. Muller has noted,

> October 1973 was a critical turning point. Just as October 1929 rang down the roaring twenties, October 1973 ended the unprecedented twenty-five year period of constant post-war economic growth, expanding prosperity, and stable prices in the industrial world. . . . What has followed since is a new economic condition, a mixture of persistent stagnation, intractable unemployment, uncontrollable inflation, and periodic recession (Muller, 1980, pp. 17-19).

Additionally, the revulsion in the Administration and the Congress resulting from the invasion of Afghanistan by the Soviet Union in December, 1979, led to pressures for increasing the percentage of the national budget devoted to defense and the withdrawal by the Carter Administration of the SALT II arms control proposals. This practically removed hope for reductions in the monies allocated to the defense sector for the foreseeable future. In fact, had the defense budget proposals of the first Reagan Administration budget been reduced by only $3 billion, the total defense appropriation would have been below the last Carter budget request (Ott, 1983).

The dramatic success of the new President in gaining swift congressional approval of steep reductions in maximum individual income tax rates and the Omnibus Budget Reconciliation Act of 1981 signaled a sharp change in direction and priorities. The theory supporting deficit financing was based on the belief that if individual and corporate tax rates were reduced, more money would be available for capital investment producing economic growth and employment (Stockman, 1986). Unfortunately, the tax reform that might have diverted these dollars into more productive, longer-term investments in plants and machinery did not occur until the passage of the Bradley-Gephardt Tax Reform Act of 1986.

The period since 1981 will likely be remembered as one of the most significant in American economic history. To expand upon the military buildup of the last budgets of its predecessors, the Reagan Administration, with the cooperation of a coalition in Congress, financed the largest peacetime military buildup in United States history entirely through deficit spending. Investments in military-related matters grew sharply, while investment in education, employment, and job training declined significantly relative to their previous share of the budget (Cizik, 1984). Priorities in social programs were drastically changed, producing, *inter alia*, the explosion of student indebtedness incurred via government-subsidized loans. In 1979, 64 percent of all student financial aid came in the form of grants and work study; the remaining assistance was in the form of loans. By 1984, these percentages were exactly reversed. The hoped-for Era of the Entrepreneur devolved into the Age of Arbitrage. While Wall Street was awash with hostile takeover rumors and inside trader scandals, the nation witnessed the greatest period of corporate mergers since the Guilded Age of the 1890s. Between 1982 and 1987, total federal outlays averaged only $15 billion a year more than what Reagan requested, which accounts for only 8 percent of the accumulated deficits. Economists typically measure deficit in relationship to the gross national product (GNP), not in absolute terms. The reason for this is common sense. In just five short years the self-professed fiscally conservative Reagan Administration had, with the cooperation of Congress, run up the largest national debt in American history, larger than the cumulative deficits of the previous 200 years.

The issue of political blame over the cause of the deficits is, of course, nothing new, though through the years conservatives have tended to engage in more blame-placing than have liberals. However, this time "the story is much scarier," as business commentator John Case noted, adding that the Reagan deficits differ from their historical forbearers in three respects:

> *Size.* Economists measure government spending not in absolute terms but in relation to the GNP. That's only common sense: as GNP expands we can afford more debt, and if the debt is growing slower than the economy as a whole, we're in good shape. Under Reagan, however, the federal deficit expanded from 2.6 percent of GNP to 5.3 percent in 1986, adding more than $1 trillion in red ink to our national accounts. Worse, this growth took place not during wartime or recession, but in a period of peace and prosperity (when real GNP has increased 22 percent between 1982 and 1987). That's when the national debt is supposed to *shrink*.
>
> *Persistence.* Total government outlays between 1982 and 1987 averaged only $15 billion a year more than what Reagan requested. That accounts for only 8 percent of the accumulated deficits.
>
> *Effects.* In the past, the government financed its deficits mostly by selling bonds to American investors. This time it has borrowed from the rest of the world. The result: by the end of 1987 the United States had completed a fast transition from the world's largest creditor to the world's largest debtor, owing foreign investors roughly $400 billion. What made the

borrowing possible were high interest rates, which themselves may have been caused by the big deficits. With foreigners happy to snap up high-yielding American assets, the dollar remained high, making imports cheap and damaging the competitive position of U.S. manufacturers. We therefore ran up huge trade deficits and provided overseas investors with ever-increasing quantities of dollars to lend us (Case, 1988).

The results of the economic policies of the 1980s include the following:

(1) The greatest trade imbalance in American history at the rate of about $500 million per day in 1986, $57 billion in 1986 with Japan alone, leaving America as a debtor nation. It has been estimated that for each $1 billion lost in trade, America loses 25,000 jobs; thus, the $150 billion deficit in 1985 translated into roughly 3.7 million Americans out of work (Bruce, 1985);

(2) A collapse or near collapse in four of the key sectors that helped fuel the unprecedented American prosperity in the post-World War II era--agriculture, heavy manufacturing, mining, and textiles--as the nation's goods quickly became overvalued on the world market (Winter, 1987); and

(3) A record budget deficit that is a veritable sea of red ink--well over $20,000 owed to each and every American, a situation thought by some not likely to improve in the near future.

Communities across the United States in 1982 found themselves in the grips of the deepest recession since the Great Depression of the 1930s. The tight fiscal policies of the Federal Reserve successfully reigned in inflation--at the expense of the highest effective rates of interest since the 1930s, which particularly hit agricultural areas hard. Congress and the American people rejected in the 1982 national elections the Reagan Administration's "New Federalism" domestic policy agenda, and particularly the deep cuts proposed for aid to college students specifically and education generally. Those elections resulted in twenty-five Democratic candidates elected, the most dramatic defeat in Congress of the party in power in the White House since the 1930 national elections. In fact, President Reagan's 1983 State of the Union address did not include a single reference to the "New Federalism" proposals that had been so ballyhooed just one year before (Ehrbar, 1984). It should be noted, however, that this did not stop the Administration from substituting a nearly slavish adherence to a narrow philosophy for bipartisan policy making. *In each of the Reagan federal budgets submitted to the House, none received more than fifteen votes in any of the years between 1983 and 1987.* The obvious intransigence at the highest levels of government directly affected community colleges desirous of creatively deploying dollars from federal or federal flow-through employment assistance job training programs following the recession of the 1980s.

While total economic recovery has not occurred since 1982, it has been slow and uneven across the nation. This has been especially true for Americans living in areas dependent upon agriculture, mining, textiles, and heavy manufacturing. Agriculture, historically the most efficient and productive sector of the economy, has experienced farm foreclosure rates equal to those experienced during the Dust Bowl era of the 1930s. The lack of policies to promote reinvestment, capital formation, and reindustrialization, combined with the deficit-resulting trade imbalance, produced a loss of 95,000 textile jobs and 16,000 apparel jobs in the southeastern United States alone between 1980 and 1986. Most of the apparel jobs lost were in rural areas, where traditionally women from farm families earned vital second incomes (Winter, 1986). The decline in the mining sector directly resulted from the glut of oil and the noncompetitiveness of American coal exports due to the overvalued dollar.

American post-Vietnam War economic policies have been inconsistent, ill-planned, and ill-defined. The overall prognosis is grim at best. America is now more vulnerable than ever before in this century to external economic, social, and political forces beyond its control. Oil imports in 1987 are near the 48 percent rate of the pre-1973 OPEC cartel era. With the domestic oil industry literally shut down, and stimulus for conservation and incentives for the development of alternative energy sources removed, America is at least as vulnerable to a potential stoppage in shipments of Middle Eastern oil as it was during the gas line summers of 1973 and 1979. The fact that the Iranian Army was twenty-seven miles from the Kuwaiti border in the fall of 1987 is a perilous reality of modern times. With the $2 trillion federal budget deficits, the nation's ability to fight future recessions through traditional Keynesian economic means of "spending our way out of it" has been reduced.

It is important for community college leaders to understand the economic situation for two reasons: first, like all institutions, community colleges do not operate in isolation from the rest of society; second, community colleges will likely be challenged to do more with less. The challenge to do more with less offers a compelling reason why community leaders, and indeed public and private sector leaders at all levels, are looking to community colleges for nontraditional, pro-active assistance in economic development. The ability of community colleges to effectively respond, however, is lessened by the current set of related employment assistance/job training policies under which they must operate.

D. <u>Community Colleges and America's Human Resource Development Crisis</u>

It is within the overall context of great economic and demographic change that community, junior, and technical colleges are challenged to train the unemployed, underemployed, and currently employed needing retraining/job upgrading courses and programs. In 1989, the nation is burdened with a failed set of national employment and job training policies. As community-based institutions, community colleges have been challenged to do even more with less. Recent shifts in the labor force and current national economic development and employment/job training policies provide a framework for understanding the motivation for and direction of greater community college involvement in economic development.

Current research shows a clear mismatch of existing job training programs to current needs. Data presented below come primarily from a Report to the Committee on Labor and Human Resources, which supported Senate Bill 514 (March 20, 1987), the legislation titled "Jobs for Employable Dependent Individuals Act." According to the report:

- Nearly four million U.S. families were expected to receive Aid to Families with Dependent Children (AFDC) in 1987, a quarter of which will likely receive AFDC benefits for the *next decade*.

- There were about two million blind or disabled individuals receiving Federal Supplemented Security Income (SSI) benefits in 1987.

- The principal federal job training effort was Title II-A of the Jobs Training Partnership Act (JTPA). The JTPA program was appropriated $1.84 billion for the 1987 fiscal year, with an estimated participation level of 1,042,000 individuals for the year and an average enrollment of 324,000 individuals.

- Fewer than 150,000 of the four million AFDC recipients were enrolled in the JTPA program.

- The Work Incentive Program (WIN), funded at $115 million, provided less than $35 per welfare family per week, while child care costs average well over $60 per week.

- The President's Committee on Employment of the Handicapped found that only 9.7 percent of disabled SSI recipients were served by JTPA programs, while unemployment among disabled workers is estimated to be as high as 66 percent. (United States Senate, Committee on Labor and Human Resources).

The above data alone does not adequately describe the challenges faced by public policy-makers regarding new directions for employment/job training programs. However, the nation can and must do better to avoid decades of structural unemployment, underemployment, and worker alienation. In a society based upon work, according to labor economist Anthony P. Carnevale:

> Legal requirements that make work a *quid pro quo* for income and consumption are firmly established in our income transfer system. While participation in the culture and polity are not legally predicated on work, the normative connection between work and full participation is strong. Indeed, recognition of that normative relationship accounts for at least some share of the surge in job seeking by youths and women (Carnevale, 1984, p. 113).

Thus, transitional child care, follow-through remunerations of percentages of welfare payments, transitional medical benefits, and expanded youth employment programs should figure prominently in the policy debate over employment/job training legislation. Whether two-year colleges seize the tactical and strategic high ground now held to build local institutional incentives into federal and state policies is a matter open to debate. Changes in U.S. employment assistance/job training policies to solve America's human resource development crisis are badly needed if the nation is to progress economically and socially. As noted by Carnevale:

> In a work-based society there is no alternative to deficit reduction and the difficult terrain that lies beyond on the path toward full employment. The current arrangement is untenable. Macroeconomic policy appears incapable of driving unemployment toward acceptable levels without igniting inflation. The resultant high and permanent unemployment rates would be more acceptable if the unemployment were randomly distributed among the citizenry. Long-term unemployment concentrates among a consistent minority of female, ethnic, young and Spanish-speaking Americans. At the same time, affirmative action programs have run afoul of majority rights and the hard-won seniority and collective bargaining rights of organized labor. As a result, a minority of Americans are caught in a squeeze between disemploying macroeconomic policies initiated in the interest of price stability and majority protections under the Fourteenth Amendment. The net effect is a not very subtle form of economic triage, whereby a consistent minority sacrifices work and income in the interest of price stability and majority freedoms. The current reality is unfair in a work-based society where consumption is predicated on earned income and only those unable to work are granted unearned assistance, where the moral prerequisite for participation in the community is self-support and the ability to support one's dependents (Carnevale, 1984, p. 19).

E. Community Colleges and Shortcomings in American Political Ideology

In the previous three sections a brief discussion of demographic changes, economic trends since the post-Vietnam War era, and America's human resource development crisis were offered to provide a broad general framework regarding the factors motivating leaders in the public and private sectors to take a new look at the community college as a source of help in economic development. Several shortcomings in the prevailing American political ideology that prevent adequate addressing of the abovementioned elements, factors, and trends are considered in this section. The reason is that community colleges sit as a politically impartial helping organ committed to change. Community colleges do not operate in a vacuum. Regardless of one's sentiments, the involvement of community colleges is directly and indirectly influenced by politics and various political ideologies.

There are shortcomings with much of the prevailing American political ideology to come to grips with change. Consider these two statements:

(1) It is cheaper to pay people to work than it is to pay them to do nothing.

(2) One is either adding to the tax base or acting as a drain on it.

The United States remains the only westernized democracy that pays its temporarily unemployed workers benefits, while at the same time disallows free tuition, vouchers, or whatever that would allow these unemployed workers to become retrained and retooled. Arguably, it shows a shortsightedness, as well as a lack of compassion, for the symbolic underlying message is that one's work is unneeded and one's contribution has little worth. In a society where two people meeting for the first time typically ask each other the question, "Where do you work?", this represents a most powerful symbol. As the community college often is the neutral turf where labor, conservatives, Democrats, management, liberals, and Republicans meet, appreciating the shortcomings of political ideologies and the symbolic incongruities is of vital importance if the institution is to fully play its helping, change agent role.

Summary

Profound demographic, economic, political, and social changes since 1973 have provided impetus and motivation for private and public policy-makers to give a fresh look toward the community college as a vehicle to provide answers. There appear to be five leading causes for this phenomenon: changing demographics, post-Vietnam War economics, America's human resource development crisis, the shortcomings of the prevailing political ideology, and the growing recognition that community colleges are a delivery system already in place. Community college leaders need a broad framework to assess the impact of these longer-term changes on their local areas. The need to provide new and different services in new and different ways leads directly into the presentation of the seven models of nontraditional community college involvement in economic development.

PART THREE:

SEVEN MODELS OF NON-TRADITIONAL INVOLVEMENT BY COMMUNITY COLLEGES IN ECONOMIC DEVELOPMENT

In this section, seven diverse models of nontraditional involvement in economic development activities are presented. There are a great many more models of successful community college involvement in economic development. Clearly the efforts are as varied as the needs of the regions the 1,200 institutions serve. The diversity is there *by definition*, given the community-based mission of these institutions. The information describing the models is gathered from three sources: presentations by officials of the institutions at regional and national meetings; technical reports, brochures, institutional audits, and other information supplied by the colleges; and personal interviews. The models presented were chosen because together they reflect diversity of efforts, and in no way should it be concluded that they are the only general models of community college effectiveness in nontraditional economic development.

A. The Institute for Business and Industry at Lake Michigan College

The case of Lake Michigan College represents what a rural-based community college can do to provide important, critically needed programs and services to positively affect the economic development of its service region. Well into the mid-1980s the Benton Harbor region, located in the tip of southwest Michigan, was suffering from the lingering effects of the deep recession of 1980-82. In the summer of 1984, unemployment was in the double digits, the college's full-time enrollment had declined by 20 percent between 1981 and 1983, and part-time enrollment remained static. In short, the service area of this rural community of 150,000 people was in a state of economic disruption, as the two major sectorial sources of income, heavy industrial manufacturing and agriculture, were in decline.

Like many rural areas around the country, poor market conditions produced in part by large trade imbalances and budget deficits had created a depressed agricultural sector. The Berrien County area has a very long growing season (with twenty-seven fruits and vegetables being grown locally), and traditionally the area's productivity has been second only to California. Additionally, the heavy industrial manufacturing sector was in decline. Primarily a provider of support machinery and parts for the auto industry, the area was racked by the shocks and aftershocks of the closings of three major plants owned by Clark Equipment Company, Whirlpool Corporation, and Sheller Globe Corporation that together employed about 3,000 workers. These high-paying union jobs traditionally paid in excess of $12.00 per hour; thus the closing of these plants between 1980 and 1982 had a dramatic negative ripple effect on the rest of the region's economy.

By June of 1987, the economic situation had improved in southwestern Michigan. Unemployment was down to 7.2 percent, a rate higher than local leaders preferred, but far better than the double digit rates of 1984 and 1985. Closings of heavy industrial manufacturing plants had stopped, and the downtown of the city of Benton Harbor, population 16,000, which had been likened to that of a ghost town just a few years before, was showing signs of new life. While it is clear that external forces played an important role in turning the situation around, what the local community did for itself to stabilize the industrial base and diversify its small business sector is a model for other areas of the nation.

The Institute for Business and Industry (IBI) at Lake Michigan College has played a vital leadership role in local economic development efforts, demonstrating what a community college can do to support industrial retention and small business development. The Institute was created in October of 1984 to provide customized training to business and industry on a scale unknown to rural southwest Michigan. The Institute, as a separate department of the college, was charged with the responsibility to bring a central focus to institutional efforts to help businesses function in a more productive manner. The initial genesis of IBI was to provide customized training in statistical process control to the 30 small- and middle-sized die-cast plants in the Berrien County area. Customized training programs in group decision-making and related management techniques were soon added, as was the servicing of training needs of public sector organizations.

By March 1986, after just fourteen months of operation, IBI had provided customized training to over 3,500 managers, supervisors, and operators. By June 1987, a total of 4,500 individuals in the private and public sectors had been served. On June 30, 1987, the end of the institutional fiscal year, IBI-customized training programs had generated revenues of about $1.1 million. Expenses were about $480,000, divided between administration (including rent, phone, and salaries--$100,000), indirect costs paid to the college ($150,000), and the cost of the adjunct trainers' salaries and travel ($230,000). Of the nearly $1.1 million in generated revenue, $950,000, or 90 percent, was derived from private industry sources, and the remaining 10 percent from public grant sources including JTPA, U.S. departments of Labor, Commerce, and Education, and the state of Michigan's Business and Industrial Training Program. Thus, over a half million dollars was turned over to the general revenue fund of the institution as a return on Lake Michigan College's investment into IBI, with $177,000 more to follow two years later in delayed funding formula adjustments from the Michigan Community College Board for credits generated through IBI programs for which continuing education credits were earned.

Currently, IBI provides the following programs and services:

(1) customized training programs geared to specific business and industry needs, including the development of company-specific generic modules, individualized curricula, and heavy use of videotaping.

(2) the delivery of on- and off-campus training for managers, supervisors, and operators.

(3) consultive assistance for private and public sector agencies and organizations.

(4) special needs projects for companies and governmental agencies.

(5) grant writing assistance, including the acquisition of funds for client training.

(6) staff training/professional development training for other educational institutions and school systems.

(7) small business assistance, including assistance in the development of marketing plans and loan packages.

The development of a customized training program begins with an in-depth assessment of needs. On-site task analyses, various survey instruments, management/ supervisory questionnaires, and assessment testing are all part of the effort. Upon determining training needs, specific strategies to accomplish the training are undertaken. William J. Baker noted bluntly, "many times businesses do not know what their needs are," because they have not addressed this key issue. Generic training modules customized to the specialized needs of the firm are then developed in such a way that, with slight modifications, they can be used by the firm itself to develop further training/updating programs. The modules introduced are in most cases computerized, and continuing education credits for many of the training courses are possible. Customer satisfaction is enhanced by the inclusion of the management and work force in the needs assessment process. An extensive collection of prepackaged seminars and workshops have been developed over time covering broad topic areas such as "Communications Motivation and Influence," "General Management," "Marketing and Sales," "Job Performance Review and Appraisal," "Statistical Process Control," "Computer Usage," "Manufacturing Programs," and "Entrepreneurship." Specific program choices under the broad topic of communications includes: "What is Communications?," "Trying to Liberate a Thought," "Assertive Communications," "Listening," and "The Trust Climate." General management programs would include "Role of the Supervisor," "Delegation," "How to Be a Good Boss," and "Employee Discipline." Basically, three of the five full-time members of the IBI staff perform curriculum/training program writing, one handles fiscal operations and management, and the fifth person manages the office.

At a most provocative session of the 1986 Annual Convention of the American Association of Community and Junior Colleges, William J. Baker, the first director of IBI, presented compelling data supporting his belief that community colleges have a critically important role to play in providing training programs and services to business and industry. According to estimates of the National Commission on Secondary Vocational Education, Baker noted that in 1984 the private sector spent a total of about $200 billion on employee training, of which a third, or $67 billion, was obtained outside the firm. In 1995, the National Commission on Secondary Vocational Education estimates the private sector will spend about $600 billion annually, going outside the firm to obtain about $220 billion worth of training programs and services (NCSVE, 1986). Therefore, the need for private sector industries to seek training services in our increasingly specialized, technologically-oriented society is growing, and the trend of private businesses going outside the firm to obtain such training is likely to grow. "Here lies a tremendous opportunity for two-year colleges," noted Baker, who added that business was "willing to pay good money for quality training."

Between 1970 and 1980, over 85 percent of all new jobs created were in small businesses employing 500 or fewer employees. The smaller the size of the firm, the greater the percentage growth in the number of employees. A new director of IBI, Clyde Remmo, was appointed in November, 1986, after Baker returned to the private sector. In an extended interview in preparation for this monograph, Remmo assessed the current status of IBI, noting that "We're the only agency or organization [that] smaller firms, agencies and organizations can turn to for their training needs. Small businesses by the nature of their size lack the human resources and economies of scale necessary to assess, design, and implement training programs. What we do is probably best understood as a provider of human resource development services and programs to small businesses."

Unquestionably, IBI has had a dramatic impact on the institution, internally and externally. Externally, IBI generated more positive publicity for Lake Michigan College "than all other programs put together," said one college official. In addition to building excellent relations with the local business community, good relations with the agricultural sector have been developed as IBI tailored training development programs to improve local farm management practices. Collegial relations with the Michigan state departments of Commerce and Labor and the State Board of Education have developed, as has a rather unusual relationship with JTPA officials. Training programs under JTPA in the Berrien County area primarily are devoted to on-the-job training; thus, IBI's customized training programs in a sense are in competition with JTPA, with IBI often advising private firms how to best deploy JTPA monies. Additionally, the Michigan Department of Small Business and Industrial Training works with IBI officials on a monthly basis and has had Lake Michigan College officials explain IBI to other Michigan community colleges.

Internally, IBI has also had a strong impact. Initially, many faculty, especially those in the technical education programs, were wary of IBI. Concerns were voiced over the hiring of eight new adjunct trainers and twenty-two part-time trainers and the unrestricted ability of IBI to go outside the firm to deliver customized training programs, some of which with slight modification would become eligible for continuing education credit. While ever-increasing sums of money were delivered from IBI programs to the college general revenue fund, these monies did not directly affect and touch full-time working faculty. An internal marketing plan was therefore initiated to address what Remmo termed "a general misunderstanding of IBI's mission," as many faculty were concerned that "IBI's tail was wagging the dog." Ten percent of the return on investment from any IBI training program involving Lake Michigan College faculty was returned directly to the member's department, for use as the department saw fit.

According to Remmo, there have been four major benefits to the college from IBI, in addition to the $500,000 contribution to the budget. First, faculty in all areas (from English and history to the technical fields) participating as trainers are able to get a flavor for current practices in the private sector. Second, technical division faculty are able to receive a more direct pipeline of information regarding current trends in equipment and technology that can be translated into curriculum improvements. Third, the aforementioned departmental incentives are used by the faculty of the participating department for travel or equipment. Fourth, there is the benefit of the equipment purchased as part of the contracted training that is residually left over after program completion. "We basically have the video capability of a small television station," said Remmo, "which then becomes available to the institution."

Reflecting upon the program and implications from its success, Remmo offered several observations. The impact of the training programs on employer-employee relations has been significant. Quality circles, team building, and other collegial work place concepts borrowed from the Japanese have been integrated into the training programs. "We're applying the collegial Japanese model to the local small die-cast shops, with dramatic results." Remmo added, "What's encouraging is that owners of the plants are beginning to see the need for people development." The heavy use of videotaping with prior consent of employees is another result that has potentially important national implications. Remmo said that while estimates of functional illiteracy among adult workers at some plant sites are as high as 35 percent in this rural county, these workers can be taught through television. "People are so accustomed to viewing television that videotape has become an essential part of our training programs as a very real training device, especially for individuals who possess reading levels well below what is viewed as normal and appropriate for college students," he said. Another observation is the critical importance of IBI's functional independence within the college to promote risk-taking. "We're risk-takers, and proud of it," Remmo said, adding, "We even taught the college cabinet concepts of team building--it was well received." A new thrust is the promotion of small business assistance; if the Institute for Business and Industry is as successful in that area as it has been with customized training, the economic future of Benton Harbor is going to be bright. Clearly, this case study shows that a rural-based community college can make a positive impact on the economy of its service region.

B. **The Mid-Florida Research and Business Center, Inc. at Daytona Beach Community College**

As the decade of the 1980s began, the private and public sector leadership in the Daytona Beach region stood at a crossroads. The explosive population growth--roughly 380,000 inhabitants in the two-county service area amounting to a 17 percent increase in the past decade--made planning services and locating new businesses difficult. The area was and is one of the fastest-growing regions in the nation, yet the economic base was extremely stratified. Tilted toward the boom-and-bust tourism economy, there was a meeting of the minds among local chamber of commerce leaders, local public officials, and educators, that:

(1) economic diversification was needed, to create more higher-paying jobs, thus preventing an outflow of young people, and

(2) some agency or organization needed to step forward and commit itself to keep track of the fast-changing local economy for private and public sector planning purposes.

The Mid-Florida Research and Business Center, Incorporated (MFRBC) at Daytona Beach Community College was created to respond to these needs. The MFRBC is a wholly-owned, not-for-profit corporation whose trustees hold dual membership on the college's board, and there is a three-member executive committee comprised of the president, the vice-president for finance, and the vice-president for planning. There is also an advisory board to the MFRBC whose members include local bankers, a tax attorney, and several small businesses. It should be noted for explanatory purposes that Daytona Beach Community College has four branch campuses in its two-county service area, a head count enrollment of 36,000, an FTE of 6,300, and a nine-member board of trustees appointed by the governor of Florida and approved by the governor's cabinet.

Since its start in 1980, four major types of programs and services provided by MFRBC have evolved, including:

(1) Research networking, including regularized collection and dissemination of information;

(2) Contracted research projects for private and public sector organizations;

(3) Entrepreneurship training for the hard-core unemployed; and

(4) Assistance to small business.

The collection and dissemination of research information was considered the top priority, and Evelyn Fine, whose background was in journalism, was hired to serve as executive director of the center (Fine, 1985). The MFRBC immediately began collecting social, demographic, and economic statistics from a variety of local, state, federal, and private sources and disseminating them to the public through a steady stream of press releases. The press releases and release of research reports and other information regarding labor force changes, new businesses, unemployment, and education statistics helped position the center and the college in the public mind as a source of good information on business trends. Building this credibility with the local business community is why the college located the MFRBC in the same downtown office building that houses the Chamber of Commerce of Daytona Beach. The media responded positively to the center as a source of information, as evidenced by the frequency (twice a week is not uncommon) of local television appearances of Fine, thus reinforcing the college's vision for the center to represent its strong commitment to economic development.

The MFRBC's research networking component directly led to a second area of development, the delivery of contracted research projects to clients in the public and private sectors. Contracted research projects completed since 1980 include a research study comparing the business climates of sixteen Florida counties, a survey of employer's short- and long-range hiring needs for Volusia County (Daytona Beach), a health care impact study for a large local hospital, studies for local industrial development boards, a statewide study for the administration of the Job Training Partnership Act in Florida, institutional audits for Daytona Beach Community College and several of its sister institutions, and the development of a structure for a community-wide data base. Research specialties have been developed in tourism marketing research and the methodologies developed at MFRBC have been replicated by several organizations around the nation. In 1986, contracted research studies were conducted for twenty-five private businesses, and eight public sector agencies and organizations. Over a period of time, due to its track record, public and private sector leaders have come to look to MFRBC and the college for quality information and research, serving to strengthen and support the institution's efforts in other areas of economic development.

An exciting project currently underway is the implementation of a community-wide computer-based information network. Called DACIN, the Daytona Community Information Network, the project will allow private and public sector organizations and agencies to instantly share pooled information to improve facilities planning, location, planning of retail marketing, and provision of services. The college through MFRBC serves as the repository, and businesses and public agencies participating receive the pooled information for free on a *quid pro quo* basis. Those not pooling information will be able to participate on a subscription basis. The DACIN project will be run on a nonprofit, break-even basis, with direct computer tie-in to the college. "My belief is that in the industrial climate of today, where each and every community out there is trying to entice or 'purchase' new industries with subsidies and tax breaks, the currency is information," said Fine, MFRBC executive director. "Business and industry needs accurate, current local information, and the only way to do it," she said, "is to do it full-time, locally."

Entrepreneurship training for the hard-core unemployed is another component of the economic development effort at MFRBC. Initiated in 1981, the Readying Individuals for Successful Entrepreneurship (RISE) program provides eleven weeks of classroom training and hands-on experience designed to provide the knowledge and skills necessary to successfully manage a small business. Applicants to this JTPA-funded program are carefully selected by a screening committee whose members include several small business owners, and local bankers. Participants are also required to interview at least two persons who own businesses similar to the one they plan to start. Participants are selected on the basis of their demonstrated economically disadvantaged situation, possession of basic skills, and potential to manage a small business. The program relies heavily upon internships with private sector employers who provide suitable internship sites. The Center for Small Business Advisory Committee serves as the steering committee for the RISE program.

The curriculum includes seventy-five contact hours of entrepreneurial and management skills, 120 hours of financial management skills, eighty hours of marketing management skills, and 151 hours of internship and market research. Students learn computer skills, hear lectures from bankers and other businessmen, and have a monthly roundtable discussion covering topics of special interest. There is a heavy use of computers and visits to the internship sites by the faculty coordinator, and videotaping of program participants is used to help them see how others view them. There is also a monthly follow-up for a year after completion of the eleven-week training program.

The RISE program has been replicated by more than thirty other communities around the country, according to college officials. Currently the programs participants number about 100, which Fine notes "is the closest thing we do to a traditional program." Half of the courses are taught by regular college faculty, the other half by adjuncts, and FTE is generated. The RISE curriculum is available for replication, and Fine noted that a key factor in the success of RISE is the involvement of potential lenders as part of the participant screening process.

The RISE program is just one of the programs administered by the Center for Small Business, which is one of the components of MFRBC. Customized contracted training programs, assistance with marketing plans and loan packaging, and other kinds of small business assistance are offered. Fine noted that the RISE program has had a major impact on the college's traditional technical/occupational curriculum, as entrepreneurship concepts have been added. Also, one of the customized training courses, "Managing for Profitability," has been written into a textbook. Several years ago, the center developed a PC system for conducting and analyzing local labor market conditions and short-range projections. Copies of that system, including survey instrument and software, are also available.

Fine attributes much of the success of the program to three key factors: the climate the college offered to go out and assess and then meet the needs of business; the ability to take risks without restriction; the generalist nature of the MFRBC staff, all of whom are generalists by source of college degrees; and the economic condition of the community, characterized by growth and change.

It is clear that the $170,000 annual budget, profits from which are plowed back into operations for the following year, are monies well spent. More than 3,500 small business owners and entrepreneurs have participated in some MFRBC-sponsored workshop or seminar since 1980. The center has received state recognition and national recognition as well.

C. The Pueblo Business Assistance Network at Pueblo Community College

The recession of the early 1980s was particularly severe for the inhabitants of the three county service area of Pueblo Community College (PCC). The economy in rural southern Colorado was devastated by the nearly simultaneous closings or serious down-scalings of three major plants, the CF&I Steel Corporation, the Alpha-Beta Meat Packing Plant, and the Pueblo Army Department. Together these three manufacturing industries employed over 5,000 workers, who were accustomed to high-paying, $12-18 per hour union-scale jobs. At the height of the recession, unemployment climbed to 22 percent. Overwhelmed by the magnitude of the situation, no local organization or agency had yet taken the lead in developing a response. Pueblo Community College seized the opportunity to become a significant community leader by spearheading a movement to support small business development.

Involvement in a pro-active way in local economic development for Pueblo Community College began in May, 1983, with the opening of the Myers Center for Small Business. College officials saw that the previous heavy manufacturing base would never fully recover and that landing a large plant to bail the area out economically was simply not going to happen. The immediate challenge, however, was to prepare and train a work force that in many cases did not possess the skills and background necessary for entrepreneurship, while at the same time developing efforts to retain and stabilize what was left of the heavy manufacturing base. The mismatch in skills was obvious; in May, 1983, unemployment in the college's service region still hovered at 18.6 percent. What began as a single program soon grew into four separate, interrelated small business assistance programs.

Conceptually the Pueblo Business Assistance Network is elegant in its simplicity, turning new and existing small businesses into net exporters of goods and services beyond the southern Colorado region. "We did not want to start convenience stores," one official noted. Through increasing exports, the local economy would grow. Thus the goal of the college was to provide direct services and develop a coordinated response of other agencies and organizations to assist businesses, the Pueblo Business Assistance Network being the eventual result. There are four components to the network: (1) Myers Center for Small Business, (2) Pueblo Cooperation Office, Inc., (3) Pueblo Growth Corporation, and (4) Pueblo Business and Technology Center (Zeiss, 1984, 1987).

The Myers Center for Small Business is the original building block and centerpiece to the entire network. The center is an official activity of the college, with a director who reports directly to the president. Persons with business expertise, college faculty, and local business professionals offer one-on-one counseling, business planning assistance, and help in solving management and growth problems. Training seminars and programs, as well as workshops, are provided for a nominal $15 fee, and the initial counseling fee is $25 (often waived). The vast majority (85 to 90 percent) of all small business failures are due to poor planning, according to U.S. Small Business Administration figures cited by college officials.

According to Anthony Zeiss, president of the college, who authored the technical paper outlining the Myers Center for Small Business in 1983, "By helping potential entrepreneurs learn that their new idea will *not* succeed, we've still accomplished much. The client still has his or her family's savings, and it's likely the relatives won't lose theirs either." Thus, the center provides clients with assistance in the development of comprehensive business plans that include a marketing plan to determine the feasibility of the project, distribution, and financial plans. The financial plans are developed with the needs and interests of potential lenders in mind and have proven so successful that most of the city's loan officers, the chamber of commerce, and other institutions where business assistance would often be sought now automatically refer business start-up inquiries to the Myers Center.

In the area of educational services and programs, the Myers Center for Small Business conducted forty professional development seminars between 1983 and August, 1988, with 889 participants, according to a recent college study. Seminar topics have included: "The New Tax Laws and Your Business," "Building Your Own Advertising," "Attitudes and the Bottom Line," "Increase Sales and Profit Through Credit," "How to Get Help from a Bank," "The SBA and You," and "Writing the Business Plan." Additionally, the Myers Center recently arranged for chamber of commerce funding and development of a unique eight-part television series, which featured how to start and expand a small business, for Colorado Public Television and for marketing education teachers to use in the classroom.

As of August, 1988, 670 persons had contacted the Myers Center about starting a business, expanding a business, or requesting help with a specific business problem. Of these 670 contacts, 415 received individual counseling of up to six hours from the center's director. In June, 1987, phone survey to assess the center's effectiveness, 268 clients were called and 117 were reached, with a response rate of 43.6 percent. Of the 117 respondents, twenty-three were still considering starting a business, thirty-two stated their intention to not start a business, six had started and closed their doors, and fifty-six respondents were operating their own businesses. Thirty-one of the fifty-six were in operation prior to receiving center assistance, and twenty-five started their businesses after receiving assistance from the center. The fifty-six currently in business represented a total of 127 full-time and forty part-time jobs, the combined wages of which added to about $2.2 million annually. A very conservative multiplier of 1.9 was used by the college to estimate the total annual impact of these wages on the local economy, which amounted to about $4.1 million. Of the 117 respondents, roughly one in three successfully initiated new businesses with help from the Myers Center, and of the sixty-two respondents who had started their business either before or after receiving assistance from the center, only six were out of business. The survival rate of over 90 percent, or failure rate of about 10 percent, contrasts sharply with the studies of several small business experts, who estimate failure after five years in the 75 percent range.

Clearly, the Myers Center for Small Business had made a dramatic, direct impact on the Pueblo region. In August, 1988, unemployment was down to 8 percent--still too high, but still more than fourteen points below the staggering May 1983 figures. Meanwhile, the center has set the pace for the establishment of thirteen new small business development centers located at community and technical schools throughout Colorado. College administrators and faculty recognized the residual effects of community goodwill and report increased credit hour enrollments in the business management instructional programs. Final estimates of the overall impact found that in its five years of operation, the Myers Center for Small Business, now called the "Myers Small Business Development Center," had in all probability led to the creation of sixty-four new small businesses and to the assistance or survival of seventy-five existing small businesses, with a combined work force of 319 full-time and ninety-two part-time jobs. The direct annual salaries of these jobs were a little more than $5.5 million, with an annual total impact on the economy of about $10 million.

It should be noted that college administrators recognized the risks involved in assuming a leadership role in helping to solve their service area's unemployment. In consequence, the Small Business Center was developed around sound research, and a diligent effort was made to educate the college's internal and external clients about the value of the new service. Some faculty questioned the role of the college in economic development and some private business consultants viewed the college's new service as competition. Widespread internal and external communication and a supportive regional newspaper helped both groups to accept the college's involvement in economic development. No significant amount of state general funds were used for the development of the Myers Center.

As a result of the development of the Small Business Center, the college was uniquely suited to become deeply involved in the corporate recruitment activities of the Pueblo Economic Development Corporation. The president of the college serves on the industrial recruitment team and the college has become nationally recognized for its customized assessment and training activities. Twenty-three new light manufacturing plants representing 7,000 new jobs have been recruited to the community, and the college has risen to statewide prominence as a result of its leadership roles in small business development and in industrial assessment and training.

The Pueblo Cooperation Office, Inc., is a not-for-profit corporation that provides counseling services to new and existing entrepreneurs. Volunteers to the Cooperation Office and trained experts in their given fields help by providing technical assistance in developing the business plan, legal requirements, and other assistance. The college initiated the development of this not-for-profit corporation, which operates independently with the cooperation of the Myers Center for Small Business. Many of the volunteers are members of SCORE, and the counseling is free of charge. Many of the Myers Center for Small Business clients receive help in part from Pueblo Cooperation Office volunteers.

The Pueblo Growth Fund was initiated in large part due to the efforts of college officials. It is a private, soon-to-be-public, for-profit corporation established to provide leveraged loans and equity to start new and assist existing small businesses. Conceptually the idea was to get "old money" in the community, persons often holding large assets in the form of annuities and bonds, to invest a portion of those assets into the Pueblo business community. Initially named the "Capital Ideas Fund," the name was changed, as was the membership on its board, after it was determined that a change from private to public ownership would leverage more working capital. The overall emphasis has been on potential manufacturing concerns that would locate their primary operations or offices in Pueblo, and to provide the final leverage to get new entrepreneurs into business. Two successful companies have been in operation for five years as a result of this activity.

The Pueblo Business and Technology Center, a Control Data Corporation-inspired small business incubator, is designed to assist new and existing small businesses by providing packaged management, marketing, financing, and manufacturing programs, as well as attractive, cost-effective space and administrative services. Space is rented on a monthly basis, including office space and services, utilities, and basic support services, which include the following: computer-based entrepreneurial training, flexible single-space offices to light manufacturing, conference facilities, and a national directory listing. The Pueblo Economic Development Corporation owns and operates the Business and Technology Center, which typically serves twenty to twenty-five small business clients. Control Data operates small business incubators at other sites around the country, likely modeled after corporate small business incubation efforts tried in Europe.

Reflecting upon the overall success of the economic development initiatives, President Zeiss noted that improved productivity and greater profit is best achieved through a better trained work force. Community colleges therefore have "a critical role to play," Zeiss said, adding, "If we really believe in the community college mission to serve the needs of the population of the college service area, that mission must be flexible to meet changes, especially in a competitive world economy." At a more local level, Zeiss noted the extremely favorable reaction of the community to the college's leadership in the sphere of economic development, and said that "Pueblo Community College is the best positioned community college in the state now. Our enrollment is up, our graduates have very high job placement rates, we received the only new capital construction funds in the state this year, and we've been fortunate to receive extra funding for equipment from the Colorado Legislature and private industry. All of this activity has helped us reach our goal of having all of our occupational-oriented graduates gain employment in meaningful careers. Further, the college was recently requested by the state to increase its service area by five additional counties in southwest Colorado, largely due to its community-based and aggressive reputation."

D. **The Office Automation Center at Trident Technical College, Charleston, South Carolina**

Keeping postsecondary vocational and occupational curricula offerings current is a continual challenge for community colleges. Rapid technological advances have changed the equipment found in the workplace in a variety of areas. This has challenged community colleges in three ways:

(1) offering current, as opposed to dated, training to students attending the community college to prepare for the workplace;

(2) keeping instructional staff current in latest workplace practices through professional development programs; and

(3) providing adequate dollars for equipment and professional development in an era of scarce financial resources.

Within the postsecondary vocational curriculum offered by community colleges, few academic areas have seen greater technological advances than the traditional business office education program. Given the obvious advances in office workplace technology, including equipment and software, how can the business office education program be kept current?

The Office Automation Center (OAC) at Trident Technical College in Charleston, South Carolina, presents a possible way out of this dilemma. Conceptually OAC serves as an informational resource for local businesses, especially small businesses, and government agencies, providing a relaxed atmosphere where clients can: see the latest office automation technology; evaluate their office automation needs; compare features of the latest application software; use functioning office systems; and attend seminars and receive customized training on the equipment prior to its installation. The OAC features six model office areas that have been created with specially designed panel participation known as "Etho Space," by Herman Miller. Each of the six offices is spacious and designed to hold three to four work stations. The equipment, furniture, and partitions were paid for by the equipment vendors, while the college furnished the $200,000 overall renovation expense of this run-down, former inner-city high school. Products are displayed by thirteen local vendors for a temporary six-month period, ensuring the availability of the latest office automation technology.

The vendors actually feature their latest equipment in a setting resembling a showroom; however, no actual sales can take place in the center, and no selling is permitted in the model offices. According to Edna H. Chisena, director of OAC, the center is a learning resource or a living classroom. College faculty are trained to demonstrate and explain the use of the equipment and office systems featured there and to help evaluate client interest and market trends in the local area. Personal computers, printers, application software, furniture, telephone systems, copiers, filing systems, facsimile, word processors, and dictation systems are all featured in an attractive workplace. By rotating the equipment, the OAC will be able to provide business executive seminars on a continuous basis to show what is new and how to plan and budget for office automation. "We want people to think," said Chisena, who added that the OAC would serve as a teaching center. Often, businesses make important office automation decisions on the recommendations of costly consultants, and even more decisions are based upon plain guesswork. The result is inappropriate purchases, haphazard training for new users of equipment and software, and attendance at expensive vendor-sponsored events. Thus, the consultive services offered by OAC will serve two purposes: building a good rapport with the Charleston business community; and establishing Trident Technical College as a leading authority in the area of office automation in the southeastern South Carolina region.

Significant benefits from the Office Automation Center to the college internally have been derived. The OAC provides students with practical work experience in a realistic office setting. The appealing office setting has been enhanced by the continuous presence of paintings by local artists. In formal studies of the college's secretarial science program, students fell into one of two categories: those having little or no office experience; or those currently employed in secretarial positions in need of upgrading, especially in the area of word processing skills. Both are well served by the OAC, which provides the opportunity to work with the latest in telecommunications and software equipment. Employment opportunities are enhanced by the training and consultive services offered to local small business owners, who enjoy a trained work force ready to use the computer equipment the very day it arrives.

The original idea to create OAC came in 1979, when a grant submitted by the business education department faculty was developed. The original grant request was turned down, as were subsequent proposals, according to Chisena. "The project changed and evolved . . . first we came up with the idea to go to vendors for equipment, then we went to furniture companies for the furniture," said Chisena, who jokingly added, "Over time we were reduced to a state of begging." The phones were donated, as were the pictures and wall hangings, she said. The operating philosophy was born "out of necessity." Even the vendors pay to showcase their equipment, Chisena noted. Creative programming is planned for the future to keep the interest of local business.

The Office Automation Center is only part of an institution-wide emphasis to become a more pro-active player in local economic development. In recent years new associate degree programs have been developed in the areas of legal assistance, culinary arts technology, hotel/motel/restaurant management, and advanced manufacturing technology. Twenty-nine new certificate and diploma programs have also been added following a 1985 in-depth assessment of community needs in the three-county area around Charleston. Programs in wardrobe, construction and set design, and motion picture/film production have been added to support Charleston's growing film industry.

Trident Technical College has an active Office of Research that publishes bimonthly newsletters on economic trends in the Charleston region, has established a small business incubator, and is active in performing Jobs Training Partnership Act programs. The college has reorganized its administration, which now includes a dean of related studies, indicating the important status of developmental studies within the overall college curriculum. The college mission statement, printed in the *Trident Technical College 1986 Annual Report*, stated, "The College emphasizes marketable job skills and promotes economic development and the improvement of the quality of life in the communities it serves." The in-depth research conducted by the college shows local reflections of national trends regarding growth in service employment sectors including health services, government sectors, and local tourism.

The strategy has been successful, at least if enrollments are any indication. In the fall of 1981 college full-time equivalent (FTE) was 6,500, declining to 4,300 FTE in the fall of 1985. With the increased emphasis on economic development, directly tying programs and services to local needs, enrollment has risen for the corresponding quarter of the college calendar. In the fall of 1986, enrollment was 5,300 FTE, while enrollment was estimated to be about 6,000 FTE for the fall of 1987. The college is positioning itself to be a major provider of human resource development/training services; the Office Automation Center is just one of the many parts of this overall advancement.

E.   **Performance-Based Contracting at Florida Community College at Jacksonville**

As the United States began to deal with its massive human resource development problem, policy-makers at the local, state, and federal levels are likely to turn to community colleges. The community college represents a delivery system that is already in place, one that can be used to turn the unemployed, the adult illiterates, the single women heading families on welfare, and others into contributing members of society. Given the fact that most of the money for job training, welfare, child care, and adult literacy comes from the federal government to the states to be administered, it is useful to examine performance based contracting (PBC) already in place at Florida Community College at Jacksonville (FCCJ). This model, with its emphasis on accountability and flexibility, is in all likelihood a precursor of what the future state flow-through job training will look like when administered at the local level.

To understand exactly what performance-based contracting is, one must distinguish between "grants" and "performance contracts." Webster's Dictionary defines a grant as "give," perform as "accomplish," and contract as "agree or accept." Literally a grant awards dollars to achieve specific objectives within a given program framework. A performance contract, on the other hand, is a legal agreement to complete a specific objective or a group of objectives--or products--for which a designated fee will be paid. Grant budgets are developed and presented in terms of line item expenses required to accomplish total objectives, with overall performance measured as opposed to the delivery of specified products. Grant dollars are awarded at the project's start, or in increments during the life of the project, and any unspent dollars are usually returned to the funding source. Only indirect costs and expense support exist in the grant award.

Alternatively, funding for performance-based contracts is tied directly to the production and delivery of specific products at specified times. The contractor (in this case FCCJ) develops the specifications under which the product is developed and then delivered. This estimate of "fees due" is used to negotiate cost with the funding agency (perhaps the Jacksonville Private Industry Council, the Florida Department of Vocational Rehabilitation, or the U.S. Small Business Administration). The funding agency then sets a cost cap ("over this we will not go") for the delivered product (say, 100 placements) and then pays the fees as the products are delivered, according to the agreed-upon contractual specifications. It is the contractor who specifies the level of cost to be incurred in the delivery of the required product; in some cases revenue is accrued and maintained by the contractor (FCCJ). These dollars are not subject to the usage guidelines developed by other types of funded programs and may be used however the contractor (FCCJ) sees fit. These funds are not tied to operations funding or anything else. As FCCJ publications note, "performance contracting follows the traditional American free enterprise model whereby the college competes on the open market to produce a specific product for a specific fee."

Funding awarded through PBC can be utilized in a variety of ways that might lead to the development and delivery of the final products or outputs. While a specific training program might include course instruction and training on certain types of equipment, and these contracted activities will affect tuition receipts and FTE count, as well as equipment purchase or maintenance, *it is only the cost of producing the product that is negotiated and contracted.*

Thus, there is a level of risk in PBCs, and this risk has affected the operations, management, and organization of PBCs at FCCJ. According to Stephen Wise, vice-president for institutional advancement, when FCCJ first got into the PBC business in early 1985, a member of his resource development office staff would write the PBC, and upon reaching a negotiated agreement, responsibilities for administration would be fulfilled by the various deans of the institution. Problems soon arose, however, because of the misunderstanding on the part of the deans of the fundamental differences between PBCs and grants. The deans would tend to spend the money/profits from a budget perspective just like they would a grant, yet the actual money was not paid by the funding agency until the deliverables were received. In early 1986 the college had more than ten different projects in operation, and each project might employ a different placement counselor and a different recruitment officer and be administered by different units within a large urban community college. Thus, monitoring and financial controls were problems. "You can lose money on PBC if you're not careful," Wise noted "The funding agencies pay up only when the products are produced."

In July, 1987, the organization of performance-based contracts at the college was changed to streamline the administration and monitoring processes. Jeffery Oliver, who previously had been involved only in the writing of the PBCs, was appointed to the newly-created position of director of development and operations of performance contracting. Oliver noted that:

> The real problem was that all of the hard-money people in the academic divisions of the college had no incentives to run the PBCs efficiently, as they would be paid anyway. For example, assume that a PBC paid $220,000 for training and graduating 100 high school dropouts via the G.E.D. program. If the administration treats the PBC like a grant, a large percentage of the PBC might be spent on testing, counseling, and instruction before the delivery of the product (graduation), creating an administrative nightmare. With one office totally in charge, administrative controls and incentives are present and operations made more efficient.

Under the new structure, the director of development and operations for performance contracting reports directly to the vice-president for institutional advancement, with direct access to the president. Responsibilities include establishing policies and procedures, proposal development and presentation, contract negotiation, authorization of budgets and personnel to perform the contract, representation of the college on issues related to PBCs to the Florida Legislature, funding agencies and other interested parties, overall supervision of all PBCs and related grants, and evaluation of performance contracting structure. Under the director are four positions:

(1) a contract compliance officer, who collects data and monitors performance (product) of each project prior to the final billing by the FCCJ finance office to the funding agency;

(2) a contracts operations officer, who directs coordination between the projects and helps new projects mesh in with existing operations;

(3) a recruitment/intake officer to handle student recruitment/participant intake, eligibility determination, student orientation, placement, and test coordination; and

(4) a job placement officer to handle counseling, advising, pre-employment readiness training, job development, job placement, follow-up, and documentation.

The contract operations officer also handles all employee training, a problem that grew larger as PBC grew at the institution.

The projects themselves are quite varied, yet all deal with various aspects of human resource development. For example, project titles include "Computer Programmer Training for the Severely Disabled," "Clerical/Word Processing Training for Unemployed Women and Disabled Persons," "Child Care Training Program," "Challenge: Health and Rehabilitative Services," and "Displaced Homemaker Training." Funding sources within a given project vary as well and might include dollars from the Florida state departments of Labor, Vocational Rehabilitation, Private Industry Council, Health and Rehabilitative Services, and various federal sources. All projects are submitted and approved by the FCCJ Board of Trustees, and usually include significant in-kind contributions from the institution that are derived from FTE generated by the project enrollers. Thus, the need for coordination and specialization in administering the PBCs is obvious. Under the new structure, the same office is responsible for coordinating job placement for all contracts in operation, for example, and another for recruitment/intake. Thus, the projects now support each other, both in terms of people and dollar resources.

The benefits of involvement in PBC are obvious. Now, FCCJ is an active player in providing critically needed training programs for the most historically under-served, at a profit to the college. Presently, nine projects are in operation, with thirty-five people delivering the training, and only five of the thirty-five are funded on regular hard money as college instructors. In the fiscal year ending in June, 1986, PBC returned over $50,000 in unrestricted dollars to the college from $1.48 million worth of contracts. This does not take into account the indirect costs generated (all management staff except the director are paid out of the PBCs), the equipment purchased via the PBC for the institution, and the FTE (estimated at over $1 million for 1986) generated for FCCJ.

Perhaps the greater benefit is the ability PBC offers to enable the college to service historically disadvantaged and excluded citizens. The college with its new, streamlined organization can quickly and directly meet training needs through private and public funding agencies. "The future here is excellent," said Director Jeffery Oliver, adding, "Now I'm a salesman selling a product, and I can ensure quality. Performance contracting is certain to take off, in my opinion." The programs train more than 2,000 child care workers each year in a state-mandated twenty-hour program, provide trained word processors to more than eighty companies in Jacksonville, provided employment for severely disabled at ten local companies for computer programmers, produced a national catalog for the United States Navy, and trained officials of the Florida Department of Corrections to administer an employee assistance program, to name a few of the activities. Vice-President for Institutional Advancement Steve Wise added, "Today the college is a key player in local economic development."

F. **The Bevill Center for Advanced Technology at Gadsden State Community College (Gadsden, Alabama)**

The economic challenges and opportunities facing the eleven-county region of northeast Alabama that comprises the service area of Gadsden State Community College to a large extent mirror those of other heavy manufacturing areas around the nation. According to University of Alabama studies, Gadsden and Etowah counties, the two largest counties within the college's 200,000 population service area, are home to more than 140 manufacturing companies and 2,000 commercial businesses. With its heavy concentration of durable goods manufacturing plants and heavy industries, the Gadsden region was wracked by the recession of the early 1980s. In 1982 the region's unemployment rate reached 20 percent, and recovery from this Depression-like circumstance has proven to be long and slow. In 1985, the unemployment rate was still well into the double figures, at 13.8 percent, while in July of 1988 it stood at 7.5 percent. The Gadsden region, traditionally a center for textiles as well as steel and rubber manufacturing due to its easily accessible river transportation system and proximity to various raw materials, is still dealing with the lingering effects of the 1980-1982 recession and the reality that record federal budget deficits and national trade imbalances have made American manufactured goods non-competitive internationally. The Bevill Center for Advanced Manufacturing Technology is a concerted partnership designed to turn this situation around by developing a good industrial retention and a sound industrial recruitment program through the development of programs to retain and expand existing industry, recruit new industry, and to grow new industries locally. According to U. S. Representative Tom Bevill, who has represented his northeast Alabama congressional district since the mid-1960s, "This facility makes it possible to help this nation reduce its trade deficit. Tuesday [August 16, 1988] the trade deficit figures were announced, and we had a $12 billion deficit for the month of July. That means we are exporting jobs. The Bevill Center will help turn that around, by helping Alabama and the nation become more competitive in the world markets."

In late 1983, recognizing that the industrial base of the area was threatened by even higher unemployment, Mayor Steve Means appointed a blue-ribbon commission to study the economic potential of the city of Gadsden and Etowah County. The Gadsden Economic Development Commission was charged with the responsibility of developing "a unified approach to successful economic development." In conducting its work, the commission attempted to assess the strengths and weaknesses of the Gadsden area, including: availability of resources; local tax base; industrial recruitment efforts; strength and needs of existing industry, quality and needs of education/job training, health services, tourism, and labor relations; sources of funding for economic development; and quality of life issues. In all, the commission addressed concerns, problems, and opportunities in thirteen different areas and, following extensive deliberations, categorized more than thirty specific action items into general recommendations.

In response to the recommendations of the Gadsden Economic Development Commission, the Bevill Center for Advanced Manufacturing Technology was established to provide a focal point for job training and research, to allow for the transfer of the latest advances in manufacturing technology to industries in northeast Alabama and to foster a positive climate for industrial retention and industrial recruitment. The Bevill Center possesses a nine-member board of directors, with three representatives each from the city of Gadsden, the University of Alabama, which operates an extension and research center in Gadsden, and Gadsden State Community College, the area's local community college. Through this partnership, the Bevill Center serves as a focal point in northeast Alabama for the economic and industrial development activities of each sponsor. The goals and objectives of the Bevill center are categorized in the four areas of education and training, applied research and service, industry/community interaction, and administrative and fiscal affairs, summarized as follows:

I.   *EDUCATION AND TRAINING.* Goal: Develop an area work force skilled in advanced manufacturing processes and techniques by providing top quality education and training programs.

   Objective 1: Offer regularly scheduled classes in computer-aided design, computer numerical control machining, robotics, computer-aided inspection, and computer-integrated manufacturing as a part of the technology curricula of Gadsden State Community College.

   Objective 2: Develop and conduct customized training courses/programs for specific companies or groups of companies to meet specific needs relating to advanced manufacturing, quality, and productivity.

   Objective 3: Develop and conduct for open enrollment, and on a repetitive basis, short-duration workshops focused on specialty areas of advanced manufacturing technology.

   Objective 4: Develop and present seminars and symposia on a one-time basis that focus on specific topics of general interest within the areas of advanced manufacturing technology.

Objective 5: Develop and conduct in cooperation with the University of Alabama's College of Engineering an annual internship for the manufacturing engineering certificate program.

Objective 6: Develop and conduct customized training courses focused on specific topics of manufacturing technology for education personnel.

Objective 7: Assist with the development of articulated A.B.E.T. engineering technology curricula between Gadsden State Community College and the University of Alabama.

Objective 8: Assist University of Alabama officials in the development of undergraduate- and graduate-level engineering course offerings in Gadsden.

Objective 9: Facilitate vendor-developed training programs for users of specific machinery and software through agreements with the vendors/manufacturers.

II. *APPLIED RESEARCH/SERVICE.* Goal: Increase the productivity and competitiveness of area companies through applied and sponsored research, information exchange, and direct services designed to meet specific current and future needs.

Objective 1: Conduct for companies or groups of companies applied research projects that are designed to solve specific problems in advanced manufacturing or that implement known systems and/or equipment.

Objective 2: Develop and maintain an automated manufacturing information center and clearinghouse for information on new developments and opportunities for training/research, and develop through regular project activity state-of-the-art training aids such as manuals, charts, videos, interactive videos, films, computer programs, and books that enhance the learning process in advanced manufacturing.

Objective 3: Conduct information gathering projects for companies on subjects relating to advanced manufacturing; and using Bevill Center labs, provide direct services such as component measurement on a for-fee basis.

Objective 4: Conduct sponsored research related to the center's areas of technology concentration.

III. *INDUSTRY/COMMUNITY INTERACTION.* Goal: Develop and maintain a strong working relationship with community, industrial, and economic development organizations in Gadsden and throughout Alabama to enhance the center's effectiveness and increase the availability of industrial resources.

    Objective 1: Maintain a current needs assessment of manufacturing-based industries in Gadsden, Etowah County, and northeast Alabama.

    Objective 2: Establish an effective network of communication among industry, community, professional, and governmental entities, including maintaining a continuous linkage with Gadsden/Etowah Industrial Development Authority, establishing linkage with area economic development groups and other knowledgeable sources, developing and administering a periodic survey of industries (relative to center capabilities), maintaining an active Industrial Advisory Board, conducting advanced manufacturing technology orientation workshops annually for area chief executive officers, meeting regularly with area political/government officials, and participating in area community/professional associations.

IV. *ADMINISTRATIVE/FISCAL.* Goal: Forge and maintain a smoothly operating partnership between Gadsden State Community College, the University of Alabama, the city of Gadsden, the Tennessee Valley Authority, and the industrial community of northeast Alabama bringing the resources of each to bear on identified obstacles to economic growth and stability.

    Objective 1: Develop a list of resources/capabilities that each partner can provide to the center.

    Objective 2: Clearly define the role of partners relative to the agreement and mission of the center.

    Objective 3: Annually review and update mission/goals/objectives.

V. *FISCAL PLANNING AND PROGRAMMING.* Goal: Develop and implement fiscal and operational plans and procedures that provide the resources necessary to accomplish the goals and objectives of the center.

    Objective 1: Work with partners and the state of Alabama to identify a permanent line-item support structure for the center.

    Objective 2: Secure short-term support for identified staffing needs and for new equipment and facility upgrades.

    Objective 3: Develop annual strategic operating plans.

VI. *PUBLIC RELATIONS.* Goal: Increase public awareness of the need for advanced manufacturing technology and center programs as a means to increased competitiveness and economic growth.

Objective 1: Develop and implement a comprehensive target marketing plan based on the needs assessment.

The Bevill Center for Advanced Manufacturing Technology is conceptually modeled after exemplary programs such as The Center for Productivity, Innovation, and Technology at Chattanooga State Community College, Tennessee, and efforts underway at Milwaukee Area Technical College and Minneapolis Community College. The Bevill Center was designed to train workers in state-of-the-art industrial technology, using computers to design parts and to control the machines that make them, according to Director Frank Bankson.

Each of the three partners has a lead role in its respective area of expertise. Gadsden State Community College plays the lead role in providing customized training and retraining programs as well as providing coursework leading to the associate degree in new high technology programs, including electrical engineering technology, with specializations in industrial electronics and robotics, mechanical engineering (CAD/CAM), electrical technical/automated manufacturing, and machine shop technology/advanced manufacturing technology. The University of Alabama takes the lead in providing research support, implementing new engineering design systems or plans at a given industrial site, flexibility studies, cost-savings studies, and other research support where needed, employing where possible a team approach. The city of Gadsden takes the lead responsibility for identifying the needs of existing industry, surveying problems and needs, developing an ongoing needs assessment and response program including data network maintenance, and developing plans supporting the recruitment of new business and expansion of existing businesses in the Gadsden area. The University of Alabama plays a support role, offering more specialized training and research-based programs that go beyond the resources of either of the other two partners.

Congressman Bevill and his staff played a pivotal role in assisting the three-way partners by helping to secure a $1.3 million grant from the Tennessee Valley Authority (TVA) in 1987 and a second $1.3 million grant in 1988. Part of the reason for this large commitment from TVA was the willingness of the city, the community college, and the research university to invest their own resources into the project. Each of the three partners committed $200,000 per year for three years in operating costs for the Bevill Center; this hard-dollar funding commitment demonstrated to external grantmakers that the project had substance and staying power. Because the partners between them covered the initial operating costs, the TVA grants were devoted almost exclusively to equipment purchases. George Beaube, who served as interim chairman of the Bevill Center Board of Directors and recently retired as dean of Gadsden State's Technical Division after a long and distinguished career in Alabama education, said, "We need to be training people for what technology is going to be five years from now .... We're trying to train people to accept and be receptive to change. For instance, the center will train people in hydraulics, pneumatics, mechanical engineering; even welding is going to be laser and water devices." Bevill Center Director Bankson added that "the cooperative efforts of these three entities will give the area a manufacturing technology center like no other in the country."

Organizationally, the director of the Bevill Center reports to a nine-member board of directors comprised of three representatives from each of the three partners. Within the Bevill Center, there is a research coordinator, who is a full-time paid employee of the University of Alabama; a training coordinator, who is a full-time employee of Gadsden State Community College, and an external relations coordinator, whose salary is paid by the Bevill Center. There are four instructors for the following functional program areas: CAD/CAM; robotics; computerized numerical control; and automated inspection. There is also a computer systems manager, who has two assistants, and three secretarial/clerical support staff. There are also several adjunct instructors and seminar leaders from both Gadsden State Community College and the University of Alabama who teach on a regular basis. During its first year, the Bevill Center trained 124 Gadsden State Community College students in advanced manufacturing technology-based curricula, as well as 200 business and professional people. More than 3,000 people participated in equipment demonstrations and tours during the first year of operation.

The Bevill Center has had problems in this inter-institutional partnership, but some problems were going to be inevitable, several interviewees noted, when two levels of postsecondary educational institutions were brought together. But by bringing these two levels together, as well as two levels of the work force, the Bevill Center is developing partnerships of a different sort, with potential national significance. University of Alabama Gadsden Center Research Coordinator Greg Bennett noted that:

> Traditionally postsecondary vocational training has focused on training students to become technicians, competent with very specialized machinery. At the same time, engineering colleges at universities have trained professional engineers to understand broad, general concepts about how a floor operates. Both think the other's perspective is wrong; here at the Bevill Center we're trying to merge two divergent theories of education and training. Additionally by involving both technicians and engineering/business professionals in the field, working together, we're helping to bridge the gap between the engineering systems that are designed at one level and carried out at another.

As an example, he noted that engineering students can spend summers at the Bevill Center, working with university faculty, technical instructors from the community college, and professional engineers from the field, as well as students training to become technicians at Gadsden State Community College. "It's more than matching courses, it's matching concepts," Bennett added.

Mary Jolley, director of economic and community affairs at the University of Alabama, and a member of the Bevill Center Board of Directors, noted the important focus the center can bring to the community regarding technology. Jolley stated that:

> Other educational institutions from kindergarten through graduate school have the opportunity to become more familiar with technology and how it impacts on their lives. If this high technology training center can revitalize Gadsden's industrial base, it will likely prove to be a model for the entire state, for Alabama is the most heavily industrialized state in the Deep South. This would indeed be new and different.

Three other aspects of the Bevill Center program are noteworthy. First is the involvement of the Alabama State Department of Postsecondary Education, the equivalent of the state board of community colleges. The Bevill Center will serve as the state's center for the training of postsecondary vocational instructional faculty in its specialty areas mentioned above. Second, after the 1990 fiscal year, plans are to transfer permanent ownership and operational control of the Bevill Center from the center's board of directors to the direct control of Gadsden State Community College and the Alabama State Department of Postsecondary Education. Third is the efforts that have flowed from the Bevill Center to impact the area's base educational program to encourage and promote economic competitiveness. Recently, area high schools have initiated "Principles of Technology" courses in their high schools and have invested $60,000 for equipment related to teaching the program's courses. In the "Principles of Technology" program, high school students in the eleventh and twelfth grades who have completed Algebra I and are proficient in math and science participate in a series of guest lectures at the Bevill Center by faculty from the University of Alabama and Gadsden State Community College.

The Bevill Center has made a significant impact to improve the quality of postsecondary vocational instruction offered as well as the professional development of Gadsden State Community College faculty. The Bevill Center has changed the way the college organizes itself to assist with area economic development. The expanding emphasis on economic development is reflected by the creation of a new Office of Economic Development, and the appointment of Bryan Stone as its director, to develop, package and market customized training programs to business and industry. In cooperation with the Gadsden/Etowah County Industrial Development Authority, a comprehensive survey of business and industry needs has been completed, and training programs are now underway. All of the community college officials interviewed in preparation of this article have indicated that the process has evolved and at times has been difficult. While indicating that the Bevill Center Board may need slight changes to add additional community and business/industry membership, Robert Howard, president of Gadsden State Community College and the person whose brainchild led to the center, said, "The board has worked well as a model to combine the three entities to decide issues such as staffing, funds management, and the like." He added, "I believe the Bevill Center shows how a community college can assume leadership in economic development, playing a vital role in attracting new industries and supporting retention of the industrial base, by providing exposure to new techniques to improve productivity."

G. **The Center for Business and Industry at Miami-Dade Community College: The International Dimension**

The Center for Business and Industry (CBI) at the Mitchell Wolfson New World Center Campus of Miami-Dade Community College (M-DCC), Florida, offers an outstanding example of how a large, urbanized community college, located in the heart of a formerly dying central business district, can take its essential strengths and create innumerable "win-win" opportunities. Like Lake Michigan College's Institute for Business and Industry, CBI offers a comprehensive menu of prepackaged training programs and has the capability to customize its training to best meet the specific demands of a given business firm in its service region. What makes CBI unique is the international dimension: taking two of its essential strengths--geography and a multicultural, multilingual demography--to serve the training needs of firms and indeed nations beyond the borders of the continental United States.

A sample of just some of the international training programs offered by CBI would surprise many a four-year university administrator. Recent programs have included: "Human Ecology: the Person, the Family and the Community," a week-long seminar for Venezuelan psychologists and mental health professionals, delivered entirely in Spanish in Caracas; "Personnel Training for Belize," a three-week training course in office procedures and personnel practices; "Confecameras," a series of on-site courses offered through the Association of Chambers of Commerce in Bogotá, Colombia; and "American College Abroad," an ongoing program providing an associate of arts degree with an emphasis on business administration on the island of Xevis in the West Indies. Programs organized in Miami included a major three-day conference for women who own small businesses in Central and South America and two four-month training programs to provide Paraguayan professors with an overview of the latest educational technologies and teaching methodologies in mathematics and science. These are just a few of the successful training programs offered by CBI to the international business community.

While CBI was established in February of 1985, a similar program was listed among the recommendations included in the 1974 Miami-Dade Community College Self-Study. That self-study suggested the college extend educational services to business and industry professional organizations, as well as government agencies. The establishment in August 1983 of an advisory board composed of prominent community leaders helped guide the development of CBI and promoted a high level of meaningful interaction between the college and local business representatives. Thus, the establishment of CBI followed careful research of both the institutional capacity to deliver nontraditional training as well as an assessment of need out in the field. It is also important to note that from the outset CBI enjoyed the strong support of M-DCC President Robert McCabe, Wolfson Campus Vice-President Eduardo Padron, and Wolfson Campus Dean of Instruction Suzanne Richter.

Participation of faculty was enhanced through the creation of sixteen CBI Institutes, which included: Accounting, Architecture and Engineering, Banking and Finance, Computer Technology, Corporate Fitness, Foreign Trade, Hospitality Management,

Insurance, International/Intercultural Affairs, Language Communication, Legal Areas, Management and Supervisory, Marketing and Sales, Office Technology, Science Technology, and Small Business Development. Two other CBI Institutes, Career Counseling and Health Care, were added later to meet the needs of clients. These CBI Institutes served two major functions: first, to package expertise of the college faculty and staff to various external markets; second, to bring focus to the categorical training needs of business and industry within the college itself. Each CBI Institute has a core of faculty as well as consultants and advisors. This internal and external packaging, and the great attention paid by college officials to eliminate wherever possible bureaucratic impediments, has given CBI the *flexibility* it needs to be able to respond quickly and directly to the needs of the client.

An example of how the CBI executive director worked with the M-DCC business affairs division to eliminate unneeded red tape is instructive, because it is typical of the problems that other community colleges will face when considering the creation of specialized departments to broker internal college training expertise to external markets. Many business people in Miami have at one time or another graduated from or taken courses at the college. Some of these had obligations to the college such as an outstanding library book or a financial obligation that prevented the CBI from registering them in a customized course developed upon the request of their company. However, the presidents of these companies selected these individuals to participate in this specialized training. It was decided by the vice-president and the dean that all such students (with the exception of those who had outstanding federal loan obligations) whose business was paying for customized training on a flat-fee basis would be allowed to register and their obligation would be temporarily waived for that course until they decided to return to complete their degrees. The CBI staff, when encountering individuals with obligations, puts them in touch with the correct office, and those individuals usually begin to handle their obligation. This example is just one of many, and demonstrates how key administrators across the college contributed to the success of this nontraditional program. It supports the view that strong college chief executive involvement is beneficial, especially during the incubation stages of the project.

Because of the multilingual, multicultural demography of Dade County--with substantial Spanish-, Portuguese-, German-, and French-speaking peoples--it is relatively easy for CBI to find people to deliver programs in the client's language. Dade County's ethnic and linguistic diversity is reflected in the make-up of the Wolfson Campus faculty, noted CBI Executive Director Maureen O'Hara, who added, "Our versatility is our strength." While being interviewed for this monograph, O'Hara paused to take a call from the personnel director of the Spanish national telephone corporation in Madrid. As O'Hara went from Spanish to English to Spanish, negotiations ensued that will lead to the development and delivery of twenty-three different courses for 300 employees, delivered entirely in the native language.

Besides O'Hara, the Center for Business and Industry's organizational structure includes a director of training, David Lather; a full-time management consultant, Peter Diehl; a director of conferences, Isabel M. Rapp; a director of international programs,

Rafael Torrella; and two secretaries. Recent activities include yearly Business and Industry Forums, which provide local business leaders with opportunities to interact with nationally and internationally recognized business authorities, such as Tom Peters, author of *In Search of Excellence*; John Naisbett, author of *Megatrends*; Arthur Laffer, perhaps the leading "supply-side" economic theorist; and Herb Cohen, celebrated negotiator whose experience includes work with the negotiation of the release of the American hostages from Iran in 1980 and 1981. Another conference activity has been the Business Leader's Forum, where an invited group of 100 corporate members gathers three times per year to discuss economic problems and possibilities in South Florida. The forum is co-sponsored by Southeast Bank, whose senior vice-president and chief economist, J. Antonio Villamil, is an active member of the Miami-Dade Community College Foundation Board of Directors. The training is divided into two areas, domestic and international. Yet because so much of what is needed locally is in the import/export business, the two areas work closely together. Recent local training programs include "Conversational English as a Second Language" for a variety of Dade County businesses and governmental agencies; "Management Training for employees of the *Miami Herald* and Knight-Ridder Corporation; "Team Building," for the city of Miami Beach as well as the U.S. Army Recruiting, and "Tri-Ethnic Perspectives" for Burdines, Florida's largest department store chain. The local training programs are offered on a customized basis, for a specific business, or for various professional associations such as the Florida International Bankers' Association and the Miami Chapter of Life Underwriters, and on a more general cross-industry approach, such as the open-enrollment short-term courses offered on "The Paperless Office," "Introduction to Lotus 1-2-3," "DBase II," "DBase III," etc.

The background of Rafael Torrella, Director of International Programs, includes work with the United Nations, the United Nations Educational, Social, and Cultural Organization (UNESCO), and the United States Agency for International Development. Torrella came to his present position with twenty-one years of experience and many international contacts. Torrella said the potential for community colleges to offer training to international audiences, was "great," but cautioned that success must be structured. The institution must commit itself to support for its international training staff, and the kinds of periodicals needed and professional development conferences and workshops available do not neatly fit into what most community colleges support. For example, a subscription to *Development Business*, the business edition of *Development Forum* published by the United Nations, costs $300 per year. This is the "*Federal Register*" of the field, and is typically not found at most community college libraries.

Interviews with CBI staff provided advice for community colleges in two areas for those considering entry into this field. The first area concerned obtaining grants and contracts, many of which are typically sponsored by the U.S. Agency for International Development (AID). Community colleges should start small and build a good track record. Once the community college has proven it can deliver high quality training either through a contract or grant, the reputation of the institution will quickly spread by word of mouth. The CBI officials interviewed stressed the need to travel, to establish personal relationships with lay contacts in Washington and particularly within AID. Once a program is successful, momentum is easier to maintain. For example, the U.S./AID-sponsored program to train Paraguayan mathematics and science professors mentioned above was first started several years ago, and new classes came in thereafter because of the quality of the program.

The other major area of advice concerned paying attention to the technological realities and social customs of the group of individuals to be trained. An appreciation for the level of technology currently in use is particularly important for technical training programs. For example, CBI offered a training program to help Chilean shoe manufacturers, who were using manufacturing technology phased out over a decade ago in the United States, in developing export markets. To provide a meaningful experience it was vital to *understand exactly* the equipment in use and the training equipment available in Chile *before* the arrival of the CBI trainer, or the participants would leave the experience extremely frustrated. Another suggestion is to become involved personally with the students while they are here in our country. Part of the reason for the continual renewal of the Paraguayan mathematics and science professors' training program lies in the high level of personal interaction on the part of Miami-Dade Community College faculty, who made friends by inviting the Paraguayan professors to their homes for dinner and spending time with them sightseeing on weekends. "A high interpersonal touch beyond the training program itself increases the comfort level of the students and provides in many cases greater benefit than the training itself," noted CBI's Rapp. The benefits to the community college faculty from this level of interaction are obviously derived from involvement in the international dimension.

In 1987, CBI offered 204 training programs to a total of 2,231 participants, of which eight training programs had an international dimension. The CBI operates on a self-generating budget; it was estimated that the gross income of CBI to the college prior to the subtraction of the not-insignificant costs of outside consultants from funded contracts and grants was in excess of $556,000 in 1987-1988. The benefits of CBI to the faculty and the college's service area extended well beyond the dollar figures. The travel CBI offered college faculty in delivering training programs abroad was a significant benefit, while the local publicity generated helped to position the institution as a place to go for training. Finally, the benefits to the United States of having its community colleges active in the delivery of training programs is not inconsiderable, to which attention is now turned.

It is clear from the description presented above that CBI rose from the perceived need for training stated by an advisory board comprised of local Dade County citizens. Yet CBI obviously has enjoyed success in the marketing of its programs to the international business community. Executive Director Maureen O'Hara explained how the two fit together:

> Miami is considered the gateway to Latin America and the Caribbean, so it was only natural that we would take advantage of our ethnic and cultural diversity to aggressively market our institutional ability to deliver high quality training in both English and Spanish. By going international, what

we're doing is helping Miami and the area economically, by networking foreign and local business people, providing short-term practical training in the participants' native language, developing an understanding of and appreciation for cultural diversity. When a community college provides training to our international colleagues, not only is it improving the bottom line of the college . . . it is also increasing the familiarity of foreigners with American products and business methods as well as values. Our goal, then, is to constitute ourselves as a platform to project Miami's international business potential, helping others while helping ourselves.

United States Senator Paul Simon (D-Ill.) is probably the leading congressional advocate of increased funding for foreign language instruction. In his 1980 book, *The Tongue-Tied American*, Simon noted that "You can buy in any language; but to sell, you must speak the seller's language." This lesson is not important just for business, it is also critically important for educational institutions of all kinds and community colleges interested in supporting local economic development through their regular internal academic offerings and their external outreach programs. The reality of our national economy becoming a world economy suggests that community college leaders need to pay greater attention to the promotion of enrollments in foreign language instructional programs. Various commentators have suggested that the ability of first- and second-generation Americans to speak the native languages of their parents and grandparents was a contributing factor to the U.S. economic rise following World War II--and that the lack of transferring these trading skills to the third generation of the 1970s and 1980s has in part contributed to the U.S. decline. (Simon, 1980). The lesson for community colleges is clear: to promote international trade, linguistic competence is vital.

The second dimension of foreign language competence revolves around the community college's ability to impact the international community through its external outreach programs. The equivalent of the American community, junior, and technical college, with its local lay governance board independent of the state education ministry, simply does not exist in large parts of the globe. As nations in the Caribbean, Latin America, Africa, and Asia search for solutions to the crying need for a technically-trained work force to effect an improvement in their living standards, it is only natural that they would turn to the dynamic model of the community college. By offering its training programs to the international community, the Center for Business and Industry serves to bolster its service area as a major player in international trade, as well as serving as a good-will ambassador for American free enterprise abroad. National policy-makers looking for alternatives to funding costly communist counter-insurgency movements in Third World nations will likely look to America's community, junior, and technical colleges as a resource ready, willing, and able to serve the nation.

PART FOUR:

COMMUNITY COLLEGE INVOLVEMENT IN NONTRADITIONAL ECONOMIC DEVELOPMENT

Introduction

The purpose of Part Four is to provide discussion and analysis of the case studies in order to provide direction and ideas for faculty, staff, lay boards of governance, and state officials contemplating initiatives in nontraditional economic development at community colleges. A discussion of the impacts of and motivation for community college involvement in nontraditional economic development begins Part Four. This is followed by a discussion of common factors that appear to lead to success, taken from the seven selected nontraditional models presented in this monograph, and analysis of five important implications for practice that would appear to reduce potential tension and problems for those institutions entering into nontraditional economic development activities. A discussion and analysis of nontraditional economic development as it relates to the history and mission of the community college follows. Part Four concludes with an analysis of the emerging role of community colleges in economic development and presents the views and concerns of project directors and campus chief executive officers regarding nontraditional economic development and related issues. Part Four is followed by a comprehensive bibliography of economic development and community colleges, as well as related issues, to assist those contemplating their own initiatives.

A. Impacts of and Motivation for Involvement of Seven Selected Community Colleges in Economic Development: Discussion and Analysis

This section presents data regarding the impacts of and motivation for involvement by the seven selected community colleges in nontraditional economic development. The data was obtained from three sources: personal interviews with the project directors and community college chief executive officers at each of the seven selected institutions described in Part Three; surveys of the project directors and community college chief executive officers; and information obtained from institutional self-studies, promotional materials, and national presentations.

Figure One presents the impact of involvement in nontraditional economic development on the seven selected community colleges, both internal and external. It is clear that the project directors and college chief executive officers surveyed felt that there was great positive publicity coming to the institution resulting from involvement in nontraditional economic development activities. This publicity and goodwill toward the community college was reflected internally through noticeably better morale among college personnel, and externally through better understanding of institutional mission and increased financial support. In perhaps the single most important survey finding, it is clear from the survey responses and the numerous interviews with project directors and college CEOs that the lay governance board, the local state legislative delegation, and the local business community possessed a better understanding of the community college's mission due in part to institutional involvement in nontraditional economic development activities.

This finding is particularly important given the fact that the mission of the community college over a long period of time has been misunderstood by numerous higher education commentators, political observers, local, state, and federal policy-makers, and the media, as well as leaders in the private sector.

FIGURE ONE: IMPACTS OF INVOLVEMENT IN NONTRADITIONAL ECONOMIC DEVELOPMENT ON SEVEN SELECTED COMMUNITY COLLEGES

Internal to College	SA	SA	A	SA	N
The positive publicity has promoted better morale among college personnel that is noticeable.	6	6	2	0	14
The full-time faculty at my college feel threatened by the presence of nontraditional programs related to economic development on the campus.	0	4	8	2	14
The board of lay governance understands the mission of the college better in part due to the involvement of the institution in economic development activities.	3	11	0	0	14
External to College					
The efforts the college has made in economic development have produced much favorable publicity and goodwill.	9	5	0	0	14
Involvement by community colleges can have a significant, positive impact on how people work together, thus affecting the quality of products made in the college's service area.	6	8	0	0	14
Involvement by community colleges can significantly shorten the time between introduction of new manufacturing processes and products and their application on the work site.	10	2	2	0	14
My local legislative delegation understands the mission of the college better in part due to the involvement of the institution in economic development activities.	2	12	0	0	14
The publicity generated by the high-profile involvement of the college in economic development has produced increased financial support for the institution (from whatever source).	8	6	0	0	14
The business community understands what the college is about in significant measure due to involvement in economic development.	7	7	0	0	14
The general public has unrealistic expectations about what the college can really do in economic development.	0	1	12	1	14

Key: SA = Strongly Agree; A = Agree; D = Disagree; SD = Strongly Disagree; N = Number.

Regarding the statement, "The full-time faculty at my college feel threatened by the presence of nontraditional programs related to economic development on the campus," the majority of responses fell in the "disagree" and "strongly disagree" categories. Follow-up telephone interviews revealed that two of the respondents who wrote "agree" and several who responded "disagree" noted that when the nontraditional economic development program was first initiated, faculty *did* feel threatened, but that as the program and its benefits came to be better understood, full-time faculty tended to be among the strongest supporters of nontraditional economic development activities. The respondents strongly rejected the notion that the general public has unrealistic expectations about what the college can really do in economic development, and they strongly believed that the publicity generated by the high-profile involvement of the college in economic development produced increased financial support for the institution (from whatever source).

Can community colleges, through the vehicle of nontraditional economic development programs, influence the products and processes at the work site? The respondents apparently believed it was possible. There tended to be agreement or strong agreement with the statement, "Involvement by community colleges can have a significant, positive impact on how people work together, thus affecting the qualify of products made in the college's service area." There also was agreement with the statement, "Involvement by community colleges can significantly shorten the time between introduction of new manufacturing processes and products and their application at the work site." It is important to note that the nontraditional models surveyed that were *directly* geared toward improving manufacturing processes, and thus had the most experience in this area, were most strongly in agreement with this and the previously mentioned statement.

Figure Two, "Motivation for the Involvement of Seven Selected Community Colleges in Nontraditional Economic Development," presents the results of surveys of the project directors and community college chief executive officers. It is clear that the respondents hold a strong personal belief that community colleges should be intimately involved in the economic development of their service areas. Jeffery Oliver at Florida Community College at Jacksonville noted that "FCCJ takes a very pro-active view of economic development," a view echoed by project directors and college CEOs from each of the six other selected case studies.

FIGURE TWO: MOTIVATION FOR THE INVOLVEMENT OF SEVEN SELECTED COMMUNITY COLLEGES IN NONTRADITIONAL ECONOMIC DEVELOPMENT

	SA	A	D	SD	N
I believe that the economic development of the service area is central to the college's mission.	12	2	0	0	14
My faculty believe that economic development of the service area is central to the college's mission.	4	8	2	0	14
My governing board believes that the economic development of the service area is central to the college's mission.	9	5	0	0	14
The local state legislative delegation believes that the economic development of the service area is central to the College's mission.	10	4	0	0	14
Local mayors/county officials believe that the economic development of the service area is central to the college's mission.	11	3	0	0	14
The state coordinating board for community colleges/higher education believes that the economic development of the service area is central to the college's mission.	6	8	0	0	14
The local media believe that the economic development of the service area is central to the college's mission.	7	5	2	0	14
The leadership in the local private sector believes that the economic development of the service area is central to the College's mission.	8	6	0	0	14

NOTES: Survey was of project directors and community college chief executive officers from seven selected institutions involved in nontraditional economic development. The number in each category corresponds to the number of responses; the total number of responses are listed in the right hand column.

Key: SA = Strongly Agree; A = Agree; D = Disagree; SD = Strongly Disagree; N = Number.

The project directors and college CEOs perceived that their faculty agreed that area economic development was central to the college's mission, though to a slightly lesser degree than the perceived strong belief on the part of the local mayors/county officials, local state legislative delegation, and local lay governance board. An interesting finding was the respondents' belief that their state higher education coordinating boards and local media did not see economic development of the college's service region as central to the institution's mission to the same degree as did local mayors/county officials, state legislative delegation, governing board, and local private sector leadership. Perhaps the local media, who generally receive their formal education in journalism and the liberal arts, do not possess a good understanding of community college mission, and perhaps higher education coordinating boards and their staffs need to be invited to the community college to receive exposure to what these institutions can do in the area of economic development.

Regarding the impacts and effects of their respective projects, all of the project directors and college CEOs surveyed and interviewed indicated positives for students and clients served, updating and improving the relevance of the curriculum, and on faculty professional development. All indicated a positive impact on the local economy, the public relations efforts of the college, and the positioning of their institutions as active players in local economic development initiatives as a result of these projects. All of the seven project directors interviewed saw themselves and their projects as entrepreneurial risk-taking efforts. The ability to go outside the traditional structure of postsecondary vocational programs already on campus, as well as other college divisions and departments, was of critical importance to the project directors in bringing about a successful project. "Business and industry want the programs *today*, and they are quick to perceive a lack of sincerity on the part of the college administration when delays occur due to institutional turf and jurisdictional bureaucratic in-fighting," one interviewee noted. The impact on the college general revenue fund was extremely positive in three cases, a break-even proposition in one case, and a very slight loss requiring direct college subsidy in two other situations. The two legally incorporated projects simply re-invest residual profits into future operations of the projects, but both of these had significant financial impact on their institutions in terms of training equipment purchased and faculty opportunities.

All of the college presidents as well as the project directors interviewed for this monograph reported the positive impact on public relations for their institutions as a result of direct, pro-active involvement in economic development activities. The presidents provided comments similar to those of Anthony Zeiss of Pueblo Community College, who noted, "Thanks to our pro-active role in economic development, our college is better positioned in the Colorado state legislature than any in the state." Thus, the tremendous public attention focused by the involvement of institutions of higher education in economic development tends to translate into more dollar resources for the participating institution. Evelyn Fine, Director of the Mid-Florida Research and Business Center, reported that being on local television twice a week has brought a great deal of positive attention to the institution. Clearly, there are great public relations benefits for taking a pro-active position for community colleges' involvement in local economic development.

The most important outcome of community college participation in economic development activities involves the students and clients served, the local economies, and the curriculum and faculty professional development within the institution. Community colleges offering postsecondary vocational courses are responsible for providing training on up-to-date machinery to the students served. At the same time these institutions are challenged to provide more individualized instructional programs to an increasingly diverse student population; however, rapid technological changes are diminishing the ability of two-year colleges to afford the expensive machinery needed to keep students and faculty current with workplace practices. Active involvement by community colleges by definition implies in-depth research to assess local business needs. Through contact with local businesses and industries in the private sector, as well as agencies and organizations in the public sector, the scarce resources of the community college and the local businesses served can be more effectively employed. Thus, involvement in economic development activities of a nontraditional nature can open new vistas and opportunities for community colleges to be utilized to better meet community needs.

B. **Common Factors that Appear to Lead to Success in Nontraditional Economic Development: Implications for Policy and Practice**

1. **Discussion of Findings**

This section presents information derived from survey questionnaires mailed to each of the seven selected model/case study project directors and college chief executive officers, as well as interviews with key personnel at each institution closely associated with the selected nontraditional community college economic development activity. Figure Three shows the results from the survey. There was very strong agreement that the college CEO should be involved during the incubation period as well as in the periodic evaluation of the nontraditional economic development project. Survey respondents also felt that incentives to promote involvement of full-time faculty in the delivery of economic development programs are necessary and that the college should try to encourage the promotion of for-credit courses wherever possible when devising off-campus training programs. Survey respondents indicated that their institutions regularly assessed the impact of their institutions on the local economy, however, there was disagreement regarding whether tools to effectively assess the impact of college involvement in economic development programs were readily available. There was very strong support for the statement that research was critical in the development and delivery of nontraditional programs in economic development.

FIGURE THREE: KEY FACTORS THAT APPEAR TO LEAD TO SUCCESS FOR SEVEN SELECTED COMMUNITY COLLEGES INVOLVED IN NONTRADITIONAL ECONOMIC DEVELOPMENT

	SA	A	D	SD	N
There should be periodic evaluation by the college CEO of nontraditional economic development programs.	6	8	0	0	14
Our college tries to promote for-credit courses wherever possible when devising off-campus training programs.	5	5	4	0	14
Incentives to promote involvement of regular full-time faculty in the delivery of economic development programs are necessary.	7	6	1	0	14
The college CEO should be involved in the incubation of non traditional programs in economic development.	10	4	0	0	14
Tools to effectively assess the impact of college involvement in economic development are not readily available.	0	11	3	0	14
Our college regularly assesses the impact made on the economy.	6	5	3	0	14
Research is critical to delivering economic development programs.	8	6	0	0	14

NOTES: Survey was of project directors and community college chief executive officers from seven selected institutions involved in nontraditional economic development. The number in each category corresponds to the number of responses; the total number of responses are listed in the right-hand column.

Key: SA = Strongly Agree; A = Agree; D = Disagree; SD = Strongly Disagree; N = Number.

Figure Four presents information obtained from in-depth interviews with officials involved with each of the seven selected case studies of effective community college involvement in economic development. Four of the projects had formal advisory boards, two possessed a not-for-profit corporate status with its own legally incorporated board of directors, and one, the Institute for Business and Industry, organized advisory boards by the type of client industry served. Organizationally, while none of the project directors reported directly to the college chief executive officer, most of the directors sat in occasionally at the campus cabinet meetings, and all enjoyed direct access to the chief executive officer of their respective institutions. Each of the seven reported that the president was directly involved in project activities. Charles W. Branch, president of Trident Technical College, indicated that in the initial stages of project development the individual in charge of the specific project reported directly to the president, but that once the project became operational the director reported to the appropriate vice-president or dean-level administrator. This pattern was typical and would therefore seem a logical strategy for institutions planning similar efforts. It is especially important to note that *research and assessment of needs studies were conducted in all cases prior to initiating a project*, in order to improve follow-up, feedback, and quality control of each project. Also noteworthy is that all of the seven selected case studies believed their projects to be of a risk-taking, entrepreneurial nature with high public profile.

FIGURE FOUR: ORGANIZATION AND STRUCTURE, AND EFFECTS OF INVOLVEMENT FOR SELECTED COMMUNITY COLLEGES INVOLVED IN NOnTRADITIONAL ECONOMIC DEVELOPMENT

Institutions

(See Key Below)

Organization/Structure	1	2	3	4	5	6	7
Research and Needs Assessment	+	+	+	+	+	+	+
Advisory Board/Board of Directors	-	+	+	+	+	+	+
Director Reports to President	-	-	-	-	-	NA	-
Director Reports to VP/Dean	+	+	+	+	+	NA	+
Director Sits on President's Cabinet	S	S	S	-	-	-	-
Involvement/Awareness of President	+	+	+	+	+	+	+
Director Direct Access to President	+	+	+	+	+	+	+

Effects of Involvement	1	2	3	4	5	6	7
On Students/Clients Served	+	+	+	+	+	+	+
On Curriculum	+	+	+	+	+	+	+
On Faculty Professional Development	+	+	+	+	+	+	+
On College General Revenue Fund	+	BE	-	-	+	+	+
On Public Relations of College	+	+	+	+	+	+	+
Director Sees Project as Risk-taking	+	+	+	+	+	+	+
Positioning College as Player in Economic Development	+	+	+	+	+	+	+

Key to Symbols

(+) is Yes, (-) is No, (BE) is Break Even, (S) is Sometimes, and (NA) is Not Applicable.

Key to Institutions

1. Institute for Business and Industry, Lake Michigan College (MI)
2. Mid-Florida Research and Business Center, Daytona Beach Community College (FL)
3. Pueblo Business Assistance Network, Pueblo Community College (CO)
4. Office Automation Center, Trident Technical College (SC)
5. Performance-Based Contracting, Florida Community College at Jacksonville (FL)
6. Bevill Center for Advanced Manufacturing Technology, Gadsden Community College (AL)
7. Center for Business and Industry, Miami-Dade Community College (FL)

It appears from the careful examination of each of the case studies that there are five key, interrelated areas that can provide problems and tensions for community colleges engaged in nontraditional economic development activities. These areas are:

(1) program independence from the traditional college structure

(2) faculty inclusion/exclusion

(3) labor/management relations

(4) administration, boards of lay governance considerations, and the traditional liberal arts curriculum

(5) unrealistic expectations

Below, each of these five areas are discussed in depth to provide ideas and possible direction for community college leaders contemplating nontraditional economic development initiatives.

1. **Program Independence from the Traditional College Structure**

One of the obvious distinguishing characteristics of nontraditional, direct involvement by community colleges in economic development activities is the independence programs have from the traditional college structure. Faculty in some cases have little or no meaningful impact into the development of the project and its curriculum and may well jealously resent the intrusion of a new initiative that receives such great attention from the media and the public. Some deans and campus vice-presidents may also feel "left out" of the process. Additionally, the chief executive officer of the college must deal with the problem of devising appropriate controls to ensure the integrity and quality of short-term, nontraditional programs. While this is an area that deserves greater research and investigation, all seven of the models discussed in this monograph appeared to have devised controls for monitoring the progress and success of the programs.

As shown in Figures Three and Four, in order to enhance economic development in their communities, the college chief executive officers were personally involved in all seven models presented. Direct presidential involvement during the project incubation stage appears to reduce tensions among and between executive staff and faculty. Additionally, the direct involvement of the president assists in the preparation of high-quality curricula and programs, since the chief executive officer is typically quite familiar with regional, state, and professional accreditation association standards. Without the direct involvement of the college chief executive officer, the issue of program independence will likely become a major problem.

2. **Faculty Inclusion/Exclusion**

When devising specialized short courses, the seven institutions examined in this study all had the flexibility to go outside the existing institutional structure to obtain faculty and staff. At each institution some regular faculty were involved, but the ability of nontraditional community college initiatives in economic development to generate tensions appeared to be highest in this area (Gilley, 1986). One of the means of eliminating faculty apprehension regarding nontraditional programs was to create economic incentives for faculty participation in the nontraditional activities. At Florida Community College at Jacksonville, for example, faculty participation translates into dollars that are allocated by the faculty member's department to be spent as that particular department deems fit. The Center for Business and Industry at the Wolfson Campus of Miami-Dade Community College and the Institute for Business and Industry at Lake Michigan College have developed similar incentive programs to promote full-time faculty participation. Incentives were used for equipment and book purchases, as well as travel. These kinds of direct incentives are similar to the methods used to attract faculty cooperation in the development of Title III grants and other grant activities, now common at many community colleges.

3. **Labor-Management Relations**

During the post-World War II era, a number of labor institutes were established on the campuses of major universities, in many cases as a result of a direct financial contribution of a business corporation. Many of these were resented and challenged by organized labor groups, who perceived the university labor institutes as tools of big business. Community college involvement in nontraditional economic development activities needs to include organized labor representatives in the planning process of short-term learning programs and as members of the economic development advisory boards. Community colleges *must guard their well-earned reputations as neutral parties in labor-management relations*, with an interest in supporting *all* of the individuals and key groups within the service area. It appears that the best method to achieve broad-based participation is to *structure* for it in the development of key advisory committees and boards. If a given community experiences bitter labor-management conflict, it is unrealistic to expect that these tensions will not be felt during committee meetings with joint labor-management participation. Community colleges should reflect the communities they serve; and they must serve the needs of all of the community's members, not just the needs of any single group. Problems with labor-management are likely to be lessened when the community college promotes for-credit courses whenever possible while structuring customized onsite training programs for business and industry.

The authors of this study strongly feel that America must have the "world-class work force" that AACJC President Dale Parnell describes, and that community colleges can lead the way as centers for training and technology transfer application. Study after study, however, has shown that up until the early 1980s much of American heavy manufacturing industry operated on a very adversarial labor-management relations model. What is needed for the 1990s and beyond is the "renaissance technician" described by Stuart Rosenfield in a report for the Southern Technology Council (Rosenfield, 1986). To achieve this, business and organized labor will have to work more closely together to develop and support programs to train a more technologically literate work force. This means more, not less, liberal arts instruction, as well as basic adult English and in many cases expanded programs in English as a Second Language. To conclude, it is the authors' strong belief that the community college can be the resource to deal directly with America's human resource development crisis, but that this will likely never happen if there is a perception that the community college as an institution cares more about the needs of labor or business. Repeating the sad history of some of the university-based labor institutes of the 1930s and 1940s should and can be avoided.

4. **Administration, Boards of Lay Governance, and the Traditional Liberal Arts Curriculumccess**

One persistent fear of faculty at many community colleges is that an emphasis on economic development will somehow overshadow other critical educational functions, especially the humanities and liberal arts programs. This fear is likely heightened by the public statements and attention given to economic development by boards of lay governance and the central administrators they choose. One of the more enlightening aspects of the Berrien County, Michigan, project was that the local heavy manufacturing businesses recognized the importance of "people development." With the accessibility the community college provides, and the importance of more advanced learning skills to be possessed by the technical work force, this problem if creatively approached can be turned into a positive. Community college chief executive officers need to be sensitive to the relationship of the liberal arts program to democratic values and participation in the general citizenry, and CEOs must remain vigilant to those who might use the rubric of economic development to reduce this vital function within the community college. The great media attention the nontraditional economic development programs appear to receive need not overshadow the enriching liberal arts; instead, the nontraditional economic development thrust can and should increase the need if community college leaders structure their programs toward this direction. Given the rapid technological change of our present times, the adaptation and critical thinking skills to be gained from the liberal arts are of even greater long-term value to community college students. The authors believe that nontraditional economic development activities should promote student enrollments in the liberal arts courses for this reason, providing a rationale and vehicle for the "selling" of such courses to students.

5. **Unrealistic Expectations**

Closely related to the problems described above are the pressures on community college leaders to demonstrate their contributions to local and regional economic development. Given the great emphasis boards of lay governance today place on economic development when choosing a campus chief executive officer, community college leaders need to be aware of the problem of unrealistic expectations. Careful planning and needs assessment studies must be taken before proceeding with economic development programs, in order to improve the chances of success (Swanson, 1986). Quality research into the proposed project is clearly the best method to prevent the problems that are encountered as a result of unrealistic expectations of the community. As Catherine A. Rolzinski noted:

> Most higher education programs addressing economic development are "on the margin" within their institutions. They tend to be located in offices or centers that are not part of the main curricular or educational units in their institution. They usually operate in whole or in part on soft monies and remain on the "fringe" of the institution's education programs. Furthermore, institutions of higher education have a concern over compromising their central mission if these programs are brought to the core. If economic development continues to be perceived as a threat to higher education's mission and as a revenue drain, true legitimacy may never be achieved (Rolzinski, 1986, p. 8).

While Rolzinski was speaking more to a university-oriented audience, her views certainly have bearing on the community college and deserve thoughtful reflection.

C. **Nontraditional Economic Development at Community Colleges**

This section presents a discussion and analysis of nontraditional involvement by community colleges in economic development, emphasizing its relationship to the history and mission of the community college. Readers interested in reviewing how the authors characterize the differences between traditional and nontraditional economic development activities at community colleges are urged to refer to Figure One, on page 11 of this monograph.

Do nontraditional economic development programs have legitimacy as part of the community services function of a community college's mission? The recent controversy regarding auxiliary services at four-year universities and the way research universities have spun off their own wholly-owned subsidiaries demonstrate that this issue of legitimacy and mission is not a problem faced by community colleges alone. Four-year universities, particularly flagship state universities, have seen sharp challenges--often fought out on the floor of the state legislature--regarding the legitimacy of operating bookstores that not only sell books but also sell computer hardware, software, and extensive lines of clothing in direct competition with local businesses, who label such practices as "monopolistic." Likewise, research universities find themselves grappling with similar issues regarding the marketing of scientific inventions made by faculty researchers employed by the instituticn at university-owned or sponsored research facilities. How these inventions are marketed (sometimes through a wholly-owned subsidiary of the university) and how the inventors themselves are remunerated for their work demonstrates that the problems of involvement of post-secondary educational institutions in nontraditional economic development activities and tying these activities directly to mission to provide legitimacy are challenges of the first order.

How can community colleges initiating nontraditional programs promote their legitimacy within the traditional community services function of the community college mission, and is there a line somewhere out there that should not be crossed? According to Raymond J. Young, a leading community college commentator, "There does not exist anywhere a singular listing of specific services which *should be provided* (emphasis his) by a community college." Young also notes:

> The community services dimension of the community college function derives its legitimacy as does the institution itself from its educational role. A college is not after all a governing agency, a social welfare agency, a museum, a social club, an institution of religion, a voluntary association, an employment agency, a theater, or a labor union. Colleges are educational institutions. Community services are legitimate only to the extent to which they represent an extension or expansion of the educational resources directed toward the economic, social, cultural, and civic needs of the people the college serves. The college cannot always be a "prime mover" for change and its role may often be a coordinative or supportive one. It will sometimes need to assume a "partnership" role in reference to personal and community development.
>
> ... The community services program, by drawing upon its role as college-community liaison and catalyst, can provide the impetus needed for the college to focus on institutional redirection, so part of its impact will be to make the community a better one ... (Young, 1973, p. 124).

Community colleges have been involved in economic development in many cases since their founding. What distinguishes nontraditional economic development at community colleges from the more traditional vocational training programs are in large measure the location of the training, the length of the training, and the fact that community colleges themselves are acting as catalysts in reaching out to their communities, assessing and then meeting community needs. This is quite consistent with the community services functioning described by Young and others (Young, 1973).

If there is a line to be drawn, it is in distinguishing between catalyst and provider. Community college leaders, including faculty, administrators, and lay governance boards, should periodically review wholly-owned subsidiary arrangements, such as the Mid-Florida Business and Research Center at Daytona Beach Community College, to ensure proper relatedness to long-range institutional mission. It is interesting to note that the partnership between Gadsden State Community College, the city of Gadsden, and the University of Alabama will eventually be dissolve and that the Bevill Center for Advanced Manufacturing Technology will come under the ownership of the Alabama State Board of Education, the nine-member governing board for Gadsden State Community College and each of Alabama's 40 other state community, junior, and technical colleges. Business incubators, advanced manufacturing technology centers, and customized training institutes at community colleges are all commonplace; each of the models described the community college played the role of catalyst, not provider. In essence, what differentiates nontraditional economic development from the traditional vocational education offerings is that community colleges now go outside the institution to assist their communities in assessing strengths and weaknesses and in the rearranging of various pieces to produce a stronger economic whole. The legitimacy of such nontraditional economic development efforts is directly related to the community college mission, which therefore demands continuous effort on the part of college faculty, staff, and governing boards to ensure institutional integrity.

D. The Emerging Role of Community Colleges in Economic Development

In gauging the success of the seven models of institutional effectiveness in nontraditional economic development, the following key elements to success emerge. First, everyone must come to the table, cards in hand, and be willing to play them openly. *Economic development in its essence is community development*; thus if a key player, especially in a smaller community, chooses to send a proxy and sit, waiting on the sidelines for something to happen, the wait necessarily will be a long one. Cooperative partnerships as presented in the Gadsden State Community College Bevill Center model may well be the wave of the future and certainly will require broad participation to succeed.

It is clear that the primary role of community colleges will not be to facilitate direct products and processes research. This will likely remain the role of the research university, with its stronger research capabilities. Even the outstanding contract research efforts of the Mid-Florida Research and Business Center at Daytona Beach Community College are likely to be oriented toward shared informational services, as opposed to conducting basic research on new manufacturing products and processes. Additionally, community colleges must make sure that the human resource development/training programs and services they provide do not take sides on the all-important issue of job security. Programs such as "Making Unions Unnecessary" should be avoided because, while attractive to sell to small business management in the short term, they can create long-term worker alienation and mistrust between the work force and the community college. A repeat of the traditional mistrust that existed between organized labor and labor relations researchers at American colleges and universities during the post-World War II period need not be repeated in the post-Vietnam era. Further, community colleges as community-based institutions must not favor one segment of the community over another. Additionally, the community college offers much to promoting the national interest abroad, as the Center for Business and Industry at the Wolfson Campus of Miami-Dade Community College demonstrates. Clearly, the community college is a vitally important vehicle for bringing economic prosperity to all Americans in the twenty-first century.

There can be little question that the seven models of nontraditional programs offered at these community colleges have had a significant positive impact on their respective service areas. Pueblo Community College's internal program audit of the impact of the Myers Center for Small Business estimated that between the period of 1983 to 1988, the effect on the local economy was $5.5 million in direct annual salaries flowing into the southern Colorado economy. In just two years, the Institute for Business and Industry at Lake Michigan College trained well over 3,500 professional managers and 4,500 factory line workers in its southwest Michigan service region; in one year, 1987, it generated revenues of $1.1 million for the college. Florida Community College at Jacksonville estimated that its Performance-Based Contracting operation received $1.48 million in performance-based contracts in fiscal 1986, while the RISE (Readying Individuals for Successful Entrepreneurship) Program at Daytona Beach Community College has trained hundreds of recipients of Aid for Families with Dependent Children. In each of the seven models presented, the community college, through nontraditional economic development, was able to positively impact the local economy of its respective service region.

Reacting to local economic needs is an essential characteristic of the community college and is well represented in the considerable literature of the history of the community college and its mission. The 1988 Report of the AACJC Commission on the Future of Community Colleges, *Building Communities: A Vision for a New Century* (American Association of Community and Junior Colleges, 1988), recognized this, noting:

> The collaborations with employers--industries, businesses, public employers, and organized labor groups--for the training of the work force and the economic development of the community are among the most important recent developments in the community college movement. They make it possible for citizens of all ages to cope with a rapidly changing, highly technological world of work and for employers to survive in an increasingly competitive environment (p. 38).

This tie of community college mission to direct involvement in area economic development is eloquently seconded by AACJC President Dale Parnell in his provocative 1985 book, *The Neglected Majority*:

> In a nation with a moral commitment to access and opportunity, community colleges are the accessible institutions.

> In a nation with a tremendous need for skilled workers, community colleges are fulfilling that need . . . . In a nation leading in information age development, community colleges are the institutions that are helping trigger economic revitalization by matching skills to the needs of the employers. In a nation that emphasizes accountability, community colleges are a cost-effective part of higher education. In a nation deeply concerned about the quality of life, community colleges are leading the way by providing quality-of-life experiences for all levels of working men and women across this great nation (Parnell, 1985 p. 99).

It therefore should not be surprising to learn that as communities react to new economic challenges, they are increasingly turning to their community, junior, and technical colleges for new programs to meet new needs.

Figure Five, "Views and Concerns Regarding Community College Involvement in Nontraditional Economic Development and Related Issues," presents the views and concerns of the project directors and college presidents from the seven selected models of effective community college involvement in economic development. The views and concerns of these individuals are particularly instructive when considering future directions for community colleges in nontraditional economic development. There was division among the respondents with the statement that "community colleges must guard against the perception that high profile economic development programs overshadow the transfer function," as several believed that this simply was not a problem. There was strong agreement with the statement that community colleges should promote the certification of part-time instructors and trainers delivering off-campus training, as well as the statement that "performance-based contracting as a means to deliver training services is a good idea that should be expanded." There was strong agreement with the statement often attributed to AACJC President Parnell that America cannot achieve a "world-class work force" without the involvement of its community colleges, and similar agreement with the statement that national job training programs should promote the community college as a prime delivery agent of training. There was strong disagreement with the statement that "community-based organizations generally do a better job of delivering training and retraining services than do community colleges."

FIGURE FIVE: VIEWS AND CONCERNS REGARDING COMMUNITY COLLEGE INVOLVEMENT IN NOnTRADITIONAL ECONOMIC DEVELOPMENT AND RELATED ISSUES

	SA	A	D	SD	N
Community colleges must guard against the perception that high profile economic development programs overshadow transfer function.	1	7	6	0	14
Community colleges need to promote the certification of part-time instructors/trainers delivering off-campus training.	7	7	0	0	14
Community-based organizations generally do a better job of delivering training and retraining services than do community colleges.	1	0	5	8	14
Performance-based contracting as a means to deliver training services is a good idea that should be expanded.	9	5	0	0	14
National job training programs should promote the community college as a prime delivery agent of training.	11	3	0	0	14
America cannot achieve a "world-class work force" without the involvement of its community colleges.	11	3	0	0	14
If the number of affordable child care slots available on my campus could be increased by 100, there would be no problem filling them.	7	7	0	0	14
I am concerned that the changes proposed in the welfare, child care, and job training programs at the federal level have not significantly involved community colleges in program planning.	8	5	1	0	14
Federally-subsidized child care facilities on my campus would be of great positive benefit to promote the economic development of our students/citizenry.	8	6	0	0	14
National policy makers should involve community colleges in the development of technology transfer legislation.	10	4	0	0	14
The National Science Foundation does not adequately take the needs of community college students into account when devising programs to expand the nation's technological base.	8	3	3	0	14
The state land-grant/flagship university has been helpful to this college in the development of nontraditional economic development programs.	2	0	6	6	14

University officials have a good understanding of what community colleges can do in the area of economic development.	0	3	7	4	14

NOTES: Survey was of project directors and community college chief executive officers from seven selected institutions involved in nontraditional economic development. The number in each category corresponds to the number of responses; the total number of responses are listed in the right-hand column.

Key: SA = Strongly Agree; A = Agree; D = Disagree; SD = Strongly Disagree; N = Number.

Regarding the federal role in child care, welfare reform, and employment/job training legislation, survey respondents were concerned that recent federal initiatives have not adequately taken the needs of community colleges and their students into account. There was agreement with the need for increased federally-subsidized child care facilities on campus and strong agreement with the statement, "If the number of affordable child care slots on my campus could be increased by 100, there would be no problem filling them (assume $ was available)." There was strong agreement with the statement that federal policymakers should involve community colleges in developing technology transfer legislation, and there were mixed responses regarding whether this is happening now. There was near-unanimous strong agreement with the statement, "The National Science Foundation does not adequately take the needs of community college students into account when devising programs to expand the nation's technological base."

There was a division of opinion regarding how helpful state flagship/land grant universities were to the respective community colleges in developing their nontraditional economic development programs. The results were also mixed, tending toward disagreement, with the statement, "University officials have a good understanding of what community colleges can do in the area of economic development."

Conclusion

The emerging role of the community college as a key player in economic development seems to include the following areas:

(1) to serve as a community resource by providing human resource development and training, especially to businesses with 500 and fewer employees;

(2) to serve as a community resource for economic development planning;

(3) to serve as a community resource to collect, analyze, and distribute information on local social, cultural, and economic trends;

(4) to serve as promoters of entrepreneurship within the traditional postsecondary vocational/occupational curriculum;

(5) to serve as a pool of community resources to assist in the incubation and success of new and existing small businesses;

(6) to serve as a community resource to assist in industrial retention through the promotion of pooled information regarding new industrial processes and technologies;

(7) to serve as a helping agent with any organization or agency whose basic goals--the promotion of the quality of life through enhanced participation in economic, social, and cultural affairs--are shared; and

(8) to serve as helping agents willing to innovate and take risks to stimulate community growth and economic development as catalytic agents.

Involvement by community colleges in nontraditional economic development is clearly not going to be another passing fad. The massive human resource development/ training challenges facing the United States today demand attention. For example, estimates of adult illiteracy range from twenty-five to fifty million Americans, while employment training and transitional child care and medical assistance programs have been devised in a haphazard fashion. Given their open-door, community-based orientation, community colleges must become more active in the policy-making process, especially at the state and federal levels. Many of the reform proposals presently under consideration will be federally supported and state administered. With community colleges in most of the 435 congressional districts, active involvement in human resource policy development will help local, state, and federal policymakers recognize that an extensive delivery system for economic development is already in place, ready and willing to serve the nation.

A CONCLUDING THOUGHT: LOOK BEFORE YOU LEAP

In each of the seven selected models of community college involvement in economic development, *the project was based upon research that included a thorough assessment of local needs.* For those who are contemplating community college involvement in nontraditional economic development, it is important to note the strong positives associated with such initiatives. Suggested here is that community colleges closely examine the results of their most recent self-studies, spend the money from their internal budget on institutional research, visit other institutions, and take advantage of outside expertise, especially from the AACJC-affiliated Council of Universities and Colleges members, who are familiar with both the theoretical and practical problems and challenges that must be addressed to successfully integrate nontraditional community college economic development initiatives directly into the institutional mission. An extensive bibliography on the literature of economic development and community colleges follows, for the benefit of those considering their own initiatives.

BIBLIOGRAPHY

Books

AACJC Commission on the Future of Community Colleges. *Building Communities: A Vision for a New Century*. Washington, D.C.: American Association of Community and Junior Colleges, 1988.

Abram, R.; Ashley, W.; Faddis, C.; and Wiant, A. *Preparing for High Technology: Programs That Work*. Research and Development Series No. 229. Columbus, Ohio: The National Center for Research in Vocational Education, The Ohio State University, 1982.

Abram, R.; and Landrum, B. *Preparing for High Technology: 30 Steps to Implementation*. Research and Development Series No. 232. Columbus, Ohio: The National Center for Research in Vocational Education, The Ohio State University, 1982.

Alfred, Richard L. ed. *Institutional Impacts on Campus, Community, and Business Constituencies*. New Directions for Community Colleges, No. 38. San Francisco: Jossey-Bass, 1982.

American Association of State Colleges and Universities. *Issues in Higher Education and Economic Development*. Edited by Helen Roberts. Washington, D.C.: American Association of State Colleges and Universities, 1986.

Arns, Kathleen F. ed. *Occupational Education Today*. New Directions For Community Colleges, No. 3. Sponsored by the ERIC Clearinghouse for Junior Colleges. Edited by Arthur M. Cohen and Florence B. Brawer. San Francisco: Jossey-Bass, 1981.

Ashley, W.; Knopka, E; and Carrico, L. *Preparing for High Technology: Robotics Programs*. Research and Development Series No. 233. Columbus, Ohio: The National Center for Research in Vocational Education, The Ohio State University, 1983.

Blocker, C. E.; Plummer, W.; and Richardson R. C., Jr. *The Two-Year College: A Social Synthesis*. Englewood Cliffs, New Jersey, Prentice-Hall, 1965.

Brick, Michael. *Forum and Focus for the Junior College Movement*. New York: Teachers College Press, 1965.

Bogue, Jesse P. *The Community College*. New York: McGraw-Hill, 1950.

Burnett, Collins W. ed. *The Community Junior College: An Annotated Bibliography*. Columbus, Ohio: College of Education, The Ohio State University, 1968.

Bushnell, D. S. *Organizing for Change: New Priorities for Community Colleges*. New York: McGraw-Hill, 1973.

Carnevale, Anthony Patrick. *A Society Based on Work.* Columbus, Ohio: The National Center for Research in Vocational Education, The Ohio State University, 1984.

Conant, J. B. *Thomas Jefferson and the Development of American Public Education.* Berkeley and Los Angeles: University of California Press, 1963.

Chmura, Tom; Waldhorn, Steve; Gollub, Jim; Henton, Doug; Kelley, Robert; Lyman, Ted; Melville, John; and Scogin, Hal. *The Higher Education-Economic Development Connection: Emerging Roles for Public Colleges and Universities in a Changing Economy.* Public Policy Center, SRI International. Washington, D.C.: American Association of State Colleges and Universities under a cooperative agreement with the Economic Development Administration, U. S. Department of Commerce, 1986.

Cohen, Arthur M.; Palmer, James C.; and Zwemer, K. Diane. *Key Resources on Community Colleges: A Guide to the Field and Its Literature.* San Francisco: Jossey-Bass, 1986.

Cohen, Arthur M. and Brawer, Florence B. *The American College.* San Francisco: Jossey-Bass, 1982.

Cohen, Arthur M.; Lombardi, John; and Brawer, Florence B. *College Responses to Community Demands.* Assisted by Joanne Frankel, Leslie Purdy, and the staff of the ERIC Clearinghouse for Junior Colleges, University of California, Los Angeles. San Francisco: Jossey-Bass, 1975.

Dale, Roger. ed. *Education, Training and Employment: Towards A New Vocationalism?* New York: Pergamon Press, 1985.

DeLellis, Anthony J. ed. *Rural Success: Case Studies of Successful Employment and Training Programs in the United States.* Richmond: Virginia Commonwealth University, Center for Public Affairs, September 1983.

De Vore, P. W. *Technology and the New Liberal Arts.* Cedar Falls, Iowa: University of Northern Iowa, 1976.

Diener, Thomas. ed. *Growth of an American Invention: A Documentary History of the Junior and Community College Movement.* Contributions To The Study Of Education, Number 16. New York: Greenwood Press, 1986.

Dyrenfurth, M. J. *Literacy for a Technological World.* Information Series No. 266. The National Center for Research in Vocational Education. Columbus, Ohio: The Ohio State University, 1984.

Eells, Walter C. *The Junior College.* Boston: Houghton Mifflin, 1931.

Eells, Walter C. *Why Junior College Terminal Education?* Washington, D.C.: American Association of Junior Colleges, 1941.

Faddis, C; Ashley, W.; and Abram, R. *Preparing for High Technology: Strategies for Change*. Research and Development Series No. 230. Columbus, Ohio: The National Center for Research in Vocational Education, The Ohio State University, 1982.

Friedman, Benjamin M. *Day of Reckoning: An Insider's Account of the Policies and the People*. New York: Oxford Press, 1988.

Galbraith, John Kenneth. *Money: Whence it Came, Where it Went*. Boston: Houghton Mifflin, 1975.

Gleazer, Edmund J., Jr. *The Community College: Values, Vision, and Vitality*. Washington, D.C.: American Association of Community and Junior Colleges, 1980.

Gleazer, Edmund J., Jr. *Project Focus: A Forecast Study of Community Colleges*. New York: McGraw-Hill Book Company, 1973.

Harrison, Bennett and Bluestone, Barry. *The Great U-Turn: Corporate Restructuring and the Polarization of America*. Boston: Basic Books, 1988.

Hispanic Higher Education Coalition. *Status Report: Hispanics in American Higher Education*. Washington, D.C.: Hispanic Higher Education Coalition, Winter 1983.

Hodgkinson, Harold L. *All One System: Demographics of Education- Kindergarten Through Graduate School*. Washington, D.C.: Institute for Educational Leadership, 1985.

Johnson, B. Lamar. *Islands of Innovation Expanding: Changes in the Community College*. Beverly Hills, California: Glencoe Press, 1969.

Johnston, William B. and Packer, Arnold E. *Workforce 2000: Work and Workers for the Twenty-first Century*. Indianapolis, IN: Hudson Institute, June 1987.

Koos, Leonard V. *The Junior College*. Vols. 1 and 2. Minneapolis: University of Minnesota Press, 1924.

Koos, Leonard V. *The Junior College Movement*. Boston: Ginn, 1925.

Kopecek, Robert J. and Clarke, Robert G. eds. *Customized Job Training for Business and Industry*. New Directions For Community Colleges, No. 48. Sponsored by the ERIC Clearinghouse for Junior Colleges. Edited by Arthur M. Cohen and Florence B. Brawer. San Francisco: Jossey-Bass, 1984.

Lemons, C. D. *Education and Training for a Technological World.* Information Series No. 267. Columbus, Ohio: The National Center for Research in Vocational Education. The Ohio State University, 1984.

Levin, H. M. *Education and Jobs in a Technological World.* Information Series No. 265. Columbus, Ohio: The National Center for Research in Vocational Education. The Ohio State University, 1984.

Long, James P. et al. *Economic Development And The Junior College.* Columbus, Ohio: The National Center for Research in Vocational Education, The Ohio State University, 1984.

Lund, Duane. *The Role of Vocational Education in the Economic Development of Rural Areas.* Columbus, Ohio: The National Center for Research in Vocational Education, The Ohio State University, 1980.

Mahoney, James R. *Community College Centers for Contracted Programs: A Sequel to Shoulders to the Wheel.* Washington, D.C.: American Association for Community and Junior Colleges, 1982.

Medsker, Leland. *The Junior College: Progress and Prospect.* New York: McGraw-Hill, 1960.

Miller, Bob W. *Higher Education and the Community College.* 2nd Edition. New York: University Press Of America, 1984.

Mitzel, David P. ed. *Resource Development in the Two-Year College.* Washington, D.C.: National Council for Resource Development, 1988.

Muller, Ronald E. *Revitalizing America: Politics For Prosperity.* New York: Simon and Schuster, 1980.

Naisbitt, John. *Megatrends.* New York: Warner Books, 1982.

National Commission on Secondary Vocational Education. *The Unfinished Agenda: The Role of Vocational Education in the High School.* National Center for Research in Vocational Education. Columbus, Ohio: Ohio State University, 1984.

National Education Association. *Universal Opportunity for Education Beyond the High School.* Washington D.C.: Educational Policies Commission, National Education Association, 1964.

Niskanen, William A. *Reaganomics: An Insider's Account of the Policies and the People.* New York: Oxford Press, 1988.

Olivas, M. A. *The Dilemma of Access: Minorities in Two-Year Colleges.* Washington, D.C.: Howard University Press, 1979.

Parnell, Dale. *The Neglected Majority.* Washington, D.C.: Community College Press, 1985.

Patten, W. G. *A Pilot Study: Priorities in Administrative Needs and Program Services for Community and Area Technical Colleges. Emphasis on Large Urban Areas.* Columbus, Ohio: National Center for Research in Vocational Education, Ohio State University, 1979.

Peters, Thomas J.; and Waterman, Robert H., Jr. *In Search of Excellence: Lessons from America's Best-Run Companies.* New York: Harper and Row, 1982.

Powers, David; Powers, Mary F.; Betz, Frederick; and Aslanian, Carol B. *Higher Education in Partnership with Industry: Opportunities and Strategies for Training, Research, and Economic Development.* San Francisco: Jossey-Bass, 1988.

Rarig, Emory W., Jr. ed. *The Community Junior College: An Annotated Bibliography.* New York: Teachers College Press, 1966.

Rudolph, F. *Curriculum: A History of the American Undergraduate Course of Study Since 1636.* San Francisco: Jossey-Bass, 1977.

Rumberger, R. W. *The Job Market for College Graduates: 1960-1990.* Palo Alto, California: Institute for Research on Educational Finance and Governance. School of Education, Stanford University, 1983.

Sher, Jonathan P. ed. *Education in Rural America: A Reassessment of Conventional Wisdom.* Foreword by Robert Coles. Boulder, Colorado: Westview Press, 1977.

Simon, Paul. *The Tongue-Tied American: Confronting the Foreign Language Crisis.* New York: Continuum, 1980.

Striner, H. E. *The Reindustrialization of the United States: Implications for Vocational Education Research and Development.* Columbus, Ohio: The National Center for Research in Vocational Education (1981).

Stockman, David A. *The Triumph of Politics: How The Reagan Revolution Failed.* New York: Harper and Row, 1986.

Stubblebine, Craig and Willett, Thomas D. eds. *Reagonomics: A Midterm Report.* San Francisco: Institute for Contemporary Studies, 1983.

U. S. President's Commission on Higher Education. *Higher Education for American Democracy.* Washington, D.C.: U. S. Government Printing Office, 1947. 6 Vols.

U. S. Senate. 100th Congress, 1st session. Committee on Labor and Human Resources. "Jobs for Employable Dependent Individuals Act." Report 100-20.

Wegmann, R. G. *Reemployment Assistance for Laid-Off Workers*. Information Series No. 258. Columbus, Ohio: ERIC Clearinghouse on Adult, Career, and Vocational Education. The National Center for Research in Vocational Education, The Ohio State University, 1983.

Weidenbaum, Murray. *Rendezvous with Reality: The American Economy after Reagan*. Boston: Basic Books, 1988.

Weintraub, Sidney and Goodstein, Marvin. eds. *Reaganomics in the Stagflation Economy*. Philadelphia: University of Pennsylvania Press, 1983.

Articles, Reports, and Presentations

American Association of Community and Junior Colleges. "Responding to the Challenge of a Changing American Economy: 1985 Progress Report on the Sears Partnership Development Fund." Washington D. C.: Association of Community College Trustees, 1986.

American Association of Community and Junior Colleges. "Putting America Back to Work: The Kellogg Leadership Initiative. A Report and Guidebook." Sponsored by Kellogg Foundation, Battle Creek, Michigan. Washington, D.C.: American Association of Community and Junior Colleges, March 1984.

American Association of State Colleges and Universities. "Business and Higher Education: Imperative to Adapt." In *Issues in Higher Education and Economic Development*. Washington, D.C.: American Association of State Colleges and Universities, 1986.

Astarita, S. "Economic Impact in Rural Delaware." *Community and Junior College Journal,* 43, no. 8 (1973): 26-29.

Barton, T. E. et al. "High-Technology Training at Greenville Technical College." Greenville, S.C.: Greenville Technical College, 1984.

Bator, Francis M. "America's Inflation." In *Reaganomics in the Stagflation Economy*, pp. 3-14. Edited by Sidney Weintraub and Marvin Goodstein. Philadelphia: University of Pennsylvania Press, 1983.

Borquist, Bruce. "The Community College Approach to Serving Business and Industry." *Community Services Catalyst,* 16, no. 4 (Fall 1986): 19-21.

Boyd-Beauman, Fran and Piland, William E. "Illinois, Arizona Find Great Resources in Colleges." *Community and Junior College Journal*, 54, no. 3 (November 1983): 18-20.

Brown, S. M. "Primer for Colleges Who Intend to Provide Training in Industry." Haverhill, Massachusetts: Northern Essex Community College; and Boston: Massachusetts State Commission on Postsecondary Education, 1981.

Bruce, Terry. Hearings of the U. S. House Higher Education Subcommittee on National Higher Education and Economic Development Act of 1985. Spring 1985.

Burger, Lynn Tolle. "The Progress of Partners." *Community and Junior College Journal* 55, no. 3 (November 1984): 28-30.

Bushnell, David S. "Articulating with Industry in Economic Development." In *Occupational Education Today*. New Directions For Community Colleges. No. 33, pp. 31-42. Edited by Kathleen F. Arns. Sponsored by the ERIC Clearinghouse for Junior Colleges. Edited by Arthur M. Cohen and Florence B. Brawer. San Francisco: Jossey-Bass, 1981.

Campbell, Dale F. and Faircloth, D. M. "State Models for Economic Development." *Community and Junior College Journal,* 52, no. 7 (April 1982): 18-19.

Case, John. "Reagan's Economic Legacy," *Inc. Magazine*, Vol. 10, No. 10, October, 1988, pp. 31-33.

Chapman, Charles E. "Ohio Joins the Club." *Junior College Journal,* 35 (October 1964): 8-12.

Cizik, Robert. "The Challenge of Less Government." In *Reaganomics: The New Federalism*, pp. 19-26. Edited by Carl Lowe. The Reference Shelf, Vol. 55, No. 5. New York: The H. W. Wilson Company, 1984.

Clary, Joseph R. and Iverson, Maynard J. *Maximizing Responsiveness to Industry by North Carolina Technical and Community Colleges. Occupational Education Research Project. Final Technical Report*. Raleigh: Department of Occupational Education, North Carolina State University, 1983.

Cresci, Gerald D. "Predicted Growth in Junior Colleges." *California Education,* 2, no. 6 (February 1965): 21-22.

Cutler, Edward. "Open for Business." *Community and Junior College Journal,* 55, no. 3 (November 1984): 28-30.

Decker, Richard C. "The Ohio Network for Information Exchange: Past, Present and Future." Paper distributed at Annual Convention of American Association of Community and Junior Colleges. November 1987.

Delta College, University Center, Michigan. "The Impact of Community Colleges on Michigan and Its Economy." January 1984.

Duncan, G. and Hoffman, S. "The Incidence and Wage Effects of Overeducation." *Economics of Education Review* 1 (Winter 1981): 75-86.

Duscha, Steve. "Retooling for Productivity." *Community and Junior College Journal,* 55, no. 3 (November 1984): 40-42.

Eckelberry, R. H. "Editorial Comment: Ohio Needs Community Colleges." *Educational Research Bulletin,* 40, No. 1 (January 11, 1961): 19-21.

Edge, Barbara and MacDonald, William J. "Profitable Partnerships: Public-Private Partners in Economic Development." Paper presented at the Annual Conference of the Council for Advancement and Support of Education (Alexandria, Virginia, December 9-11, 1986).

Ehrbar, A. F. "Reagan Steps Back from Reaganomics." In *Reaganomics: The New Federalism*, pp. 156-163. Edited by Carl Lowe. The Reference Shelf, Vol. 55, No. 5. New York: The H. W. Wilson Company, 1984.

Eldersveld, A. Martin. "Pennsylvania Opens the Door." *Junior College Journal* 35 (February 1965): 9-11.

Erickson, Clifford G. "Multi-Campus Operation in the Big City." *Junior College Journal,* 35 (October 1964): 17-20.

Eskow, Seymour. "Putting America Back to Work: Phase II." *Community and Junior College Journal,* 54, no. 3 (November 1983): 12-14.

Eskow, Seymour. "The Community College and the Human Resources Development Council: Toward a National Training Strategy for the United States." Unpublished paper, 1982.

Fine, Evelyn. "Small Business Resource Center: Providing the Means to Success." In James R. Mahoney and Clyde Sakamoto (Eds.), *International Trade Education: Issues and Programs*. Washington, D.C.: American Association of Community and Junior Colleges, National Center for Higher Education, 1985.

Fretwell, E. K., Jr. "New York: The Next Five Years." *Junior College Journal,* 33 (March 1963): 22-25.

Fox Valley Technical Institute. "Fox Valley Technical Institute Economic Development Plan." Appleton, Wisconsin: Fox Valley Technical Institute, 1984.

Garrison, Don C. "Keeping America Working: On Time, and Winning." *Community and Junior College Journal,* 55, no. 7 (April 1985): 54-56.

Gilley, J. Wade. "Back to the Future: Education and Economic Development Continue a Symbiotic Relationship in America." Presented at the National Conference on Higher Education and Economic Development. Atlanta, Georgia: April 21, 1986.

Gleazer, Edmund J., Jr. "AAJC Approach." *Junior College Journal*, 33 (April 1963): 3-4.

Goodwin, Gregory L. "A Social Panacea: A History of the Community-Junior College Ideology." In T. Diener (Ed.), *Growth of an American Invention: A Documentary History of the Junior and Community College Movement*. New York: Greenwood Press, 1986.

Graham, Walter A. "It May Happen in Alabama, Too." *Junior College Journal* 35 (November 1964): 28-29.

Greene, Elizabeth. "Colleges Hard-Pressed to Meet Demands for Child Care, Funds Called Inadequate." *The Chronicle Of Higher Education* (September 25, 1985): 29.

Groff, W. H. "Computer Literacy: Data and Information Processing as the Core of the High-Technology Information Society." Paper presented at the 1982 Great Lakes Regional Conference of American Technical Education Association, November 3-5, 1982.

Grubb, W. N. "The Bandwagon Once More: Vocational Preparation for High Tech Occupations." *Harvard Educational Review,* 54, no. 4 (November 1984): 429-451.

Harper, William A. "West Florida's New Two-Year University." *Junior College Journal,* 37 (September 1966): 13-15.

Harris, Edward. "Management Model for Economic Development." Springfield, Illinois: Illinois Development Council, 1984.

Hecker, D. "The Class of '77 One Year After Graduation." *Occupational Outlook Quarterly,* 26 (Summer 1982): 8-33.

Hodgkinson, Harold L. "Chapter Eleven: Establishing Alliances with Business and Industry." In *Issues for Community College Leaders in a New Era*, pp. 222-231, edited by George B. Vaughan et al. San Francisco: Jossey-Bass, 1983.

Holdworth, Rebecca W. "No Shrinking Violet." *Community and Junior College Journal,* 55, no. 3 (November 1984): 24-27.

Illinois Community Colleges Board. "Economic Development Grant Report, Fiscal Year 1986." Springfield, Illinois., October 1986.

Illinois State Board of Education. Department of Adult, Vocational and Technical Education. "Management Model for Economic Development." Springfield, Illinois: Illinois Development Council, 1984.

Indiana State Commission for Higher Education. "Roles for Postsecondary Education in the Economic Development of Indiana. Annual Report by the Commission for Higher Education to Governor Robert D. Orr and the Indiana General Assembly." Indianapolis: Indiana State Commission for Higher Education, January 1982.

Israel, Cary A. and Custer, Harriet H. "Making Economic Development Work: A Systematic Approach to Contract Training." *Community Services Catalyst* 16, no. 4 (Fall 1986): 16-18.

Jacobs, James. "Small Business and Economic Development in Macomb County." Warren, Michigan: Macomb Community College, Center for Community Studies, June 1983.

Jellison, Holly M. ed. *Small Business Training: A Guide for Program Building*. Washington, D.C.: National Small Business Training Network, American Association of Community and Junior Colleges, 1983.

Johnson, Berman E. "Merging Studies in Liberal Arts With High Technology: A Challenge for the Late 1980s." *Community College Journal For Research And Planning*, Fall/Winter 1986, Volume 5, No. 2, pp. 17-28.

Jones, Steven W. and Beck, Patricia M. "On the Bricks: Partners in Progress." *Community and Junior College Journal*, 53, no. 4 (December-January 1982-1983): 24-26.

Kaplan, Marshall. "Universities, Centers and Economic Development Conversion of Rhetoric to Reality." Presented at the National Conference on Higher Education and Economic Development. Sponsored by the American Association of Colleges and Universities and The National Association of Management and Technical Assistance Centers. Atlanta, Georgia. April 1986.

Katsinas, Stephen G. "Access of Hispanic-Americans to Post-Secondary Education in Illinois: Issues, Problems, Concerns and Options." Unpublished Ph.D. Dissertation. Carbondale: Southern Illinois University, October 1985.

Kingry, Larry and Cole, Lee. "The Role of Oregon Community Colleges in Economic Development." *Community College Review*, 13, no. 2 (Fall 1985): 10-16.

Knoell, Dorothy M. "New York Challenges Its Urban Colleges." *Junior College Journal*, 37 (March 1967): 9-11.

Korim, Andrew S. "Challenges Facing Community Colleges in the 1980s." In *Occupational Education Today*. New Directions For Community Colleges. No. 33, pp. 11-20. Sponsored by the ERIC Clearinghouse for Junior Colleges. Edited by Arthur M. Cohen and Florence B. Brawer. San Francisco: Jossey-Bass, 1981.

Kuenne, Robert E. "Lessons and Conjectures On OPEC." In *Reaganomics in the Stagflation Economy*, pp. 164-174. Edited by Sidney Weintraub and Marvin Goodstein. Philadelphia: University of Pennsylvania Press, 1983.

Larkin, P. "Can Colleges and Universities Supply an Adequate Skilled Work-Force for Higher-Technology Needs in 1990? Problems, Prospects, and Policy for the Eighties." Research Report No. 82-27. Largo, Md.: Prince George's Community College, 1982.

Landrum, Bertha A. et al. "Can Community Colleges Have an Impact on Unemployment?" *Community and Junior College Journal*, 55, no. 6 (March 1985): 32-35.

Landrum, Bertha A. and Gluss, M. A. "Colleges Help Communities Vie for Payrolls." *Community and Junior College Journal*, 53, no. 7, pp. 50-51.

Learn, R. L. "A Comparison Between Business and Industry Linkage Structures in Pennsylvania Community and Junior Colleges and Those Described in the Literature." Unpublished master's thesis, Indiana University of Pennsylvania, 1983.

Linthicum, Dorothy S. "Economic Development through Education at Maryland's Community Colleges." Annapolis: Maryland State Board for Community Colleges, August 1985.

Liston, Edward J. and Ward, Cynthia V. "The Greenhouse Effect." *Community and Junior College Journal*, 55, no. 3 (November 1984): 20-23.

Long, John P. "Industry Speaks to Two-Year Colleges About High Technology." Unpublished paper, 1983.

Lynch, E. "Macomb Community College Enters the World of High Tech." *Voc Ed*, 57, no. 7 (1982): 29-31.

Maner, Arnold H. "Human Resources Development: A Unique Approach." Paper presented at a Meeting of the Association for the Advancement of Policy Research and Development in the Third World." Washington D.C., November, 1981.

Martorana, S. V. and Garland, Peter H. "Public Policy for Economic Development: The Two-Edged Sword." *Community and Junior College Journal*, 55, no. 3 (November 1984): 16-19.

McCuen, John T. "Colleges 'Incredibly Effective' in Fighting Unemployment." *Community and Junior College Journal*, 53, no. 6 (March 1983): 20-21.

McGuire, W. Gary. "Worker Education for Improved Productivity: The Role of New York State Community College Contract Courses." In *Customized Job Training for Business and Industry*. Edited by Robert J. Kopecek and Robert G. Clarke. New Directions for Community Colleges. 12, no. 4 (1984): 67-74.

Michigan Community College Presidents' Economic Development and Job Training Network Steering Committee. "Michigan Community Colleges Job Training and Retraining Investment Fund. 1983-1984 Investment Fund Projects: Impact Statement." Ann Arbor: Michigan Community Colleges Economic Development and Job Training Network, 1984.

Myran, Gunder A. "Technology Transfer: Emerging Area of Service." *Community and Junior College Journal*, 49, no. 1 (September 1978): 10-12.

National Council for Occupational Education. Task Force on the Role of Community Colleges in Economic Development. "Community Colleges and Economic Development." National Council for Occupational Education Monograph Series. Volume 3, No. 1. October 17, 1986.

Nelson, Robert E. and Piland, William E. *Organizing Small Business Programs in Community Colleges*. Urbana, Illinois: Department of Vocational and Technical Education, University of Illinois, 1982.

Niland, William P. "The Master Plan Study and Trends in California Junior Colleges." *Junior College Journal*, 31 (April 1961): 427-433.

Novak, Doyce B., Jr. and Pesci, Frank B. "Progress in Maryland." *Junior College Journal*, 33 (April 1963): 16-19.

Ott, Attiat F. "Controlling Government Spending." In *Reaganomics: A Midterm Report*, pp. 79-107. Edited by Craig Stubblebine and Thomas D. Willett. San Francisco: Institute for Contemporary Studies, 1983.

Owen, H. James. "Program Planning for Economic Development in Community and Technical Colleges." *Community Services Catalyst*, 13, no. 4 (Fall 1983): 18-23.

Packwood, Gene et al. "The Impact of Community Colleges on Michigan and Its Economy: Preliminary Technical Report." *Economic Impact Studies*. June 1982.

Palmer, Jim; Colby, Anita; and Zwemer Diane. "Sources and Information: The Community College Role in Economic and Labor-Force Development." In *Customized Job Training for Business and Industry*. Edited by Robert J. Kopecek and Robert G. Clarke. New Directions for Community Colleges. 12, no. 4 (1984): 95-107.

Parsons, M. H. "Technology Transfer: Programs, Procedures, and Personnel." Paper presented at a roundtable at the Annual Convention of the American Association of Community and Junior Colleges, New Orleans, April 24-27, 1985.

Richter, Winston Boos, Jr. "Economic Development and the American Community College: A Systems Theory Approach." Unpublished Ph.D. Dissertation. Gainesville, Florida: University of Florida, 1986.

Rogers, R. H. "Landsat Technology Transfer to the Private and Public Sectors Through Community Colleges and Other Locally Available Institutions." Phase II Program, Final Report. Ann Arbor, Michigan: Environmental Research Institute, 1982.

Rolzinski, Catherine A. "Uncommon Practice for Higher Education: Recognizing the Power of the People in Community Economic Development." Presented at the National Conference on Higher Education and Economic Development. Sponsored by the American Association of Colleges and Universities and The National Association of Management and Technical Assistance Centers. Atlanta, Georgia. April 1986.

Rosenfeld, Stuart A. "The Education of the Renaissance Technician: Postsecondary Vocational-Technical Education in the South." *Foresight: Model Programs For Southern Economic Development.* 4, No. 2 (Fall 1986): 1-27. Southern Growth Policies Board, Research Triangle Park, North Carolina.

Rosenfeld, Stuart A. "Technical and Community Colleges: Catalysts For Technology Development." *Report and Recommendations, Executive Summary, National Roundtable on Economic Development, July 16, 1987.* Sponsored by the Keeping America Working Project and the Center for Occupational Research and Development, funded by the Tennessee Valley Authority and The Sears-Roebuck Foundation.

Scott, Robert. "Proven Partners: Business, Government, and Education." *Community, Technical, and Junior College Journal,* 57, no. 3 (December-January 1986-87): 16-19.

Semans, H. H. "High School--Junior College Relations in the Sixties." *Journal of Secondary Education,* 36, no. 3 (March 1961): 171-176.

Sher, Jonathan P. "School-based Community Development Corporations: A New Strategy for Education and Development in Rural America." In *Education in Rural America: A Reassessment Of Conventional Wisdom.* Edited by Jonathan P. Sher. Foreword by Robert Coles. Boulder, Colorado: Westview Press, 1977.

Smith, Eric. "Pueblo: Fresh Achievements, Fresh Perspectives." *Colorado Business Magazine* (September 1988): 27-52.

Spanbauer, Stanley J. "Increasing College Responsiveness to Community Needs." In K. Arns (Ed.) *Occupational Education Today.* New Directions for Community Colleges, No. 33. San Francisco: Jossey-Bass, 1981.

Swanson, David H. "The Role of Higher Education in Transferring Technologies to Industry." Presented at the National Conference on Higher Education and Economic Development. Sponsored by the American Association of Colleges and Universities and The National Association of Management and Technical Assistance Centers. Atlanta, Georgia. April 1986.

Taylor, Walter M. "Bold Plans for the Bay State." *Junior College Journal,* 34 (March 1964): 24-27.

Tyler, Henry T. "California's Junior Colleges, 1975 Model." *Journal of Secondary Education,* 39, no. 8 (December 1964): 376-379.

Tyree, L. W., and McConnell, N. C. "Linking Community Colleges with Economic Development in Florida." ISHE Fellows Research Report No. 3. Tallahassee, Florida: Institute for Studies in Higher Education, 1982.

Vaughan, George B. "Historical Perspective: President Truman Endorsed Community College Manifesto." *Community and Junior College Journal,* 53 (April 1983): 1-4.

Walsh, John Patrick. "Manpower Development." *Junior College Journal,* 34 (May 1964): 8-12.

Wattenbarger, James L. "Five Years of Progress in Florida." *Junior College Journal,* 34 (October 1963): 16-18.

Whitehead, A. N. "Technical Education and Its Relation to Science and Literature." Presidential address to the Mathematical Association of England, 1917. In *The Aims of Education and Other Essays.* New York: New American Library, 1949.

Wilson, Joann. "A Study of the Relationship between Postsecondary Education and Economic Development in Selected States." Phoenix: Arizona Commission for Postsecondary Education, 1981.

Winter, William F. Chairman. *Halfway Home and a Long Way to Go.* Preliminary Report of the Commission on the Future of the South. Chapel Hill: Southern Growth Policies Board, 1987.

Winter, William F. Chairman. *Shadows on the Sunbelt: Developing the Rural South in an Era of Economic Change.* A Report of the MDC Panel on Rural Economic Development. Chapel Hill, May 1986.

Yarrington, Roger, ed. *Educational Opportunity for All: An Agenda for National Action*, pp. 141-151. In T. Diener (Ed.), *Growth of an American Invention: A Documentary History of the Junior and Community College Movement*. New York: Greenwood Press, 1986.

Young, A. M. "Recent Trends in Higher Education and Labor Force Activity." *Monthly Labor Review*, 106 (February 1983): 39-43.

Young, John A. Chairman. *Global Competition: The New Reality*. The Report of the President's Commission on Industrial Competitiveness. Volume I. Washington, D.C.: United States Government Printing Office, 1985.

Young, Raymond J. "Progress and Prospects: A Study of the Kansas City Metropolitan Junior College District." Report to the Board of Trustees of the Kansas City Metropolitan Junior College District, Kansas City, Missouri. Cambridge, Massachusetts: Arthur D. Little, 1973.

Zeiss, P. Anthony. "Local Initiative for Economic Development." Pueblo, Colorado: Pueblo Community College, April 1984.

Zeiss, P. Anthony. "Using Research To Stimulate Local Initiative For Economic Development." *Community College Journal For Research and Planning*, Spring/Summer 1987, Vol. 6, No. 1, pp. 49-55.

ABOUT THE AUTHORS

Stephen G. Katsinas received his Ph.D. in Higher Educational Administration from Southern Illinois University at Carbondale in 1985. Between 1985 and 1987 he directed the Institute of Higher Education Research and Services at the University of Alabama. Since the Fall of 1987 he has served as Assistant Director of Institutional Advancement at Miami-Dade Community College. His research interests include the history and philosophy of higher education, lay governance, economic development, and minority access to higher education.

Vincent A. Lacey received his Ph.D. in Historical Studies from Southern Illinois University at Carbondale in 1985. Since 1981 he has been Director of the Computer Assisted Instruction and Research Laboratory in the College of Liberal Arts at SIU-C. He is also an adjunct graduate faculty member in the Department of Political Science at SIU-C, teaching data management. His research interests include computer applications in education and the social sciences, economic development, data management, international and American politics, and higher education policy making.